C000091138

FRENCH SENTENCE BUILDERS
A lexicogrammar approach
Beginner to Pre-Intermediate

Copyright © G. Conti, D. Viñales and R. Jézéquel

All rights reserved
ISBN: 9798747869233

Imprint: Independently Published
Edited by Julien Barrett

 THE LANGUAGE GYM

About the authors

Gianfranco Conti taught for 25 years at schools in Italy, the UK and in Kuala Lumpur, Malaysia. He has also been a university lecturer, holds a Master's degree in Applied Linguistics and a PhD in metacognitive strategies as applied to second language writing. He is now an author, a popular independent educational consultant and professional development provider. He has written around 2,000 resources for the TES website, which have awarded him the Best Resources Contributor in 2015. He has co-authored the best-selling and influential book for world languages teachers, "The Language Teacher Toolkit" and "Breaking the sound barrier: Teaching learners how to listen", in which he puts forth his Listening As Modelling methodology. Gianfranco writes an influential blog on second language acquisition called The Language Gym, co-founded the interactive website language-gym.com and the Facebook professional group Global Innovative Language Teachers (GILT). He is also the founder and owner of the popular website, www.language-gym.com and, last but not least, Gianfranco has created the instructional approach known as E.P.I. (Extensive Processing Instruction).

Dylan Viñales has taught for 15 years, in schools in Bath, Beijing and Kuala Lumpur in state, independent and international settings. He lives in Kuala Lumpur. He is fluent in five languages, and gets by in several more. Dylan is, besides a teacher, a professional development provider, specialising in E.P.I., metacognition, teaching languages through music (especially ukulele) and cognitive science. In the last five years, together with Dr Conti, he has driven the implementation of E.P.I. in one of the top international schools in the world: Garden International School. This has allowed him to test, on a daily basis, the sequences and activities included in this book with excellent results (his students have won language competitions both locally and internationally). He has designed an original Spanish curriculum, bespoke instructional materials, based on Reading and Listening as Modelling (RAM and LAM). Dylan co-founded the fastest growing professional development group for modern languages teachers on Facebook, Global Innovative Languages Teachers, which includes over 12,000 teachers from all corners of the globe. He authors an influential blog on modern language pedagogy in which he supports the teaching of languages through E.P.I. Dylan is the lead author of Spanish content on the Language Gym website and oversees the technological development of the site. He is currently undertaking the NPQML qualification, after which he plans to pursue a Masters in second language acquisition.

Ronan Jézéquel has taught for 15 years, in schools in Frimley, Brighton and Kuala Lumpur in state and international settings. He lives in Kuala Lumpur. He is fluent in three languages, and gets by in several more. Ronan is, besides a teacher, a keen mountain biker and an outdoor enthusiast. In the last five years, together with Dr Conti and Dylan Viñales, he has contributed to the implementation of E.P.I. in one of the top international schools in the world: Garden International School. This has allowed him to test, on a daily basis, the sequences and activities included in this book with excellent results. Ronan is the lead author of French content on The Language Gym website and he also brings the competitive element from his sporty background to TLG with the design of live games and features such as our leaderboard.

 **THE LANGUAGE GYM**

Acknowledgements

Translating a book is a time-consuming yet rewarding endeavour. Ronan would like to thank his wife, Mariana, for her help and support and more importantly for being an amazing partner.

Secondly, a huge thanks to our editor, Julien Barrett, from Nantes, France. He is always a pleasure to work with; good humoured, extremely dedicated and with an eagle-eye. His contributions have gone **far** beyond proofreading for accuracy, into advising on best selection of language content, and offering inter-cultural boosts along the way. He has been a real asset to our team.

Thirdly, heartfelt thanks to Tom Ball and all the World Languages team at Garden International School, for being fantastic colleagues, and for helping to create a world class working environment, where it was possible to lay the foundations for E.P.I. and produce the bank of Sentence Builders that are the foundation for this booklet.

Lastly, a shout-out to the talented Ross Padgett, former Head of Art at Garden International School for his superb work designing the book cover.

 **THE LANGUAGE GYM**

Introduction

Hello and welcome to the first 'text' book designed to be an accompaniment to a French Extensive Processing Instruction course. The book has come about out of necessity, because such a resource did not previously exist.

How to use this book if you have bought into our E.P.I. approach

This book was originally designed as a resource to use in conjunction with our E.P.I. approach and teaching strategies. Our course favours flooding comprehensible input, organising content by communicative functions and related constructions, and a big focus on reading and listening as modelling. The aim of this book is to empower the beginner-to-pre-intermediate learner with linguistic tools - high-frequency structures and vocabulary - useful for real-life communication. Since, in a typical E.P.I. unit of work, aural and oral work play a huge role, this book should not be viewed as the ultimate E.P.I. coursebook, but rather as a **useful resource** to **complement** your Listening-As-Modelling and Speaking activities.

Sentence Builders – Online Versions

Please note that all these sentence builders will be available in bilingual and French only versions on the Language Gym website, available to download, editable and optimised for displaying in the classroom, via the Locker Room section (available via subscription).

How to use this book if you don't know or have NOT bought into our approach

Alternatively, you may use this book to dip in and out of as a source of printable material for your lessons. Whilst our curriculum is driven by communicative functions rather than topics, we have deliberately embedded the target constructions in topics which are popular with teachers and commonly found in published coursebooks.

If you would like to learn about E.P.I. you could read one of the authors' blogs. The definitive guide is Dr Conti's "Patterns First – How I teach lexicogrammar" which can be found on his blog (www.gianfrancoconti.com). There are also blogs on Dylan's wordpress site (mrvinalesmfl.wordpress.com) such as "Using sentence builders to reduce (everyone's) workload and create more fluent linguists" which can be read to get teaching ideas and to learn how to structure a course, through all the stages of E.P.I.

The book "Breaking the sound barrier: Teaching learners how to listen" by Gianfranco Conti and Steve Smith, provides a detailed description of the approach and of the listening and speaking activities you can use in synergy with the present book.

 **THE LANGUAGE GYM**

The basic structure of the book

The book contain 19 macro-units which concern themselves with a specific communicative function, such as 'Describing people's appearance and personality', 'Comparing and contrasting people', 'Saying what you like and dislike' or 'Saying what you and others do in your free time'. You can find a note of each communicative function in the Table of Contents. Each unit includes:

- a sentence builder modelling the target constructions;
- a set of vocabulary building activities which reinforce the material in the sentence builder;
- a set of narrow reading texts exploited through a range of tasks focusing on both the meaning and structural levels of the text;
- a set of translation tasks aimed at consolidation through retrieval practice;
- a set of writing tasks targeting essential writing micro-skills such as spelling, functional and positional processing, editing and communication of meaning.

Each sentence builder at the beginning of a unit contains one or more constuctions which have been selected with real-life communication in mind. Each unit is built around that construction <u>but not solely on it</u>. Based on the principle that each E.P.I instructional sequence must move from modelling to production in a seamless and organic way, each unit expands on the material in each sentence builder by embedding it in texts and graded tasks which contain both familiar and unfamiliar (but comprehensible and learnable) vocabulary and structures. Through lots of careful recycling and thorough and extensive processing of the input, by the end of each unit the student has many opportunities to encounter and process the new vocabulary and patterns with material from the previous units.

Alongside the macro-units you will find:

- grammar units: one or two pages of activities occurring at regular intervals. They explicitly focus on key grammar structures which enhance the generative power of the constructions in the sentence builders. At this level they mainly concern themselves with full conjugations of key verbs, with agreement and preposition usage. Note that these units recycle the same verbs many times over by revisiting at regular intervals but in different linguistic contexts;
- question-skills units: one or two pages on understanding and creating questions. These micro-units too occur at regular intervals in the book, so as to recycle the same question patterns in different linguistic contexts;
- revision quickies: these are retrieval practice tasks aimed at keeping the previously learnt vocabulary alive. These also occur at regular intervals;
- self-tests: these occur at the end of the book. They are divided into sections, one for less confident and one for more confident learners.

The point of all the above micro-units is to implement lots of systematic recycling and interleaving, two techniques that allow for stronger retention and transfer of learning.

 **THE LANGUAGE GYM**

Important *caveat*

1) This is a '**no frills**' book. This means that there are a limited number of illustrations (only on unit title pages). This is because we want every single little thing in this book to be useful. Consequently, we have packed a substantive amount of content at the detriment of its outlook. In particular, we have given serious thought to both **recycling** and **interleaving**, in order to allow for key constructions, words and grammar items to be revisited regularly so as to enhance exponentially their retention.

2) **Listening** as modelling is an essential part of E.P.I. There will be an accompanying listening booklet released shortly which will contain narrow listening exercises for all 19 units, following the same content as this book.

3) **All content** in this booklet matches the content on **The Language Gym** website. For best results, we recommend a mixture of communicative, retrieval practice games, combined with Language Gym games and workouts, and then this booklet as the follow-up, either in class or for homework.

4) An **answer booklet** is also available, for those that would like it. We have produced it separately to stop this booklet from being excessively long.

5) This booklet is suitable for **beginner** to **pre-intermediate** learners. This equates to a **CEFR A1-A2** level, or a beginner **Y6-Y8** class. You do not need to start at the beginning, although you may want to dip in to certain units for revision/recycling. You do not need to follow the booklet in order, although many of you will, and if you do, you will benefit from the specific recycling/interleaving strategies. Either way, all topics are repeated frequently throughout the book.

We do hope that you and your students will find this book useful and enjoyable.

Gianfranco, Dylan and Ronan

TABLE OF CONTENTS

UNIT 1
Talking about my age

In this unit you will learn:

- How to say your name and age
- How to say someone else's name and age
- How to count from 1 to 15
- A range of common French names
- The words for brother and sister

J'ai quinze ans

J'ai dix ans

J'ai six ans

J'ai trente ans

UNIT 1
Talking about my age

Je *I*	m'appelle *am called*			j'ai *I have**	un 1	an *year*
Mon frère *My brother* **Ma sœur** *My sister*	**s'appelle** *is called*	**Alexandre** **Anthony** **Annabelle** **Béatrice** **Charles** **Denis** **Émilie** **Frédéric** **Isabelle** **Joséphine** **Julien** **Marie** **Paul** **Tristan**	**et** *and*	**il/elle a** *he/she has**	**deux** 2 **trois** 3 **quatre** 4 **cinq** 5 **six** 6 **sept** 7 **huit** 8 **neuf** 9 **dix** 10 **onze** 11 **douze** 12 **treize** 13 **quatorze** 14 **quinze** 15	**ans** *years*
Author's note: in French we use the verb "avoir" [to have] to talk about age **although "J'ai quatre ans" literally means "I have four years", in English, it's translated* *as "I am four years old"*						

Unit 1. Talking about my age: VOCABULARY BUILDING

1. Match up

un an	seven years
deux ans	four years
trois ans	five years
quatre ans	six years
cinq ans	eleven years
six ans	ten years
sept ans	twelve years
huit ans	nine years
neuf ans	two years
dix ans	eight years
onze ans	one year
douze ans	three years

2. Complete with the missing word

a. J'ai _____ ans. *I am fourteen years old.*

b. Mon frère _____ appelle Frédéric.

  My brother is called Frédéric.

c. Je _____ Denis. *My name is Denis.*

d. Mon frère _____ deux ans. *My brother is two.*

e. Ma sœur a _____ ans. *My sister is four.*

f. _____ m'appelle Anne. *My name is Anne.*

quatre	a	s'
je	quatorze	m'appelle

3. Translate into English

a. J'ai trois ans

b. J'ai cinq ans

c. J'ai onze ans

d. Il a quinze ans

e. Elle a treize ans

f. Il a sept ans

g. Mon frère

h. Ma sœur

i. Elle s'appelle

4. Broken words

a. J'_____ *I have*

b. Je m'ap_____ *My name is*

c. Ma s_____ *My sister*

d. Qui_____ *Fifteen*

e. Se_____ *Sixteen*

f. On_____ *Eleven*

g. Ne_____ *Nine*

h. Quato_____ *Fourteen*

i. Do_____ *Twelve*

5. Rank the people below from oldest to youngest as shown in the example

Michel a quinze ans	1
Marie a treize ans	
Francis a deux ans	
Paul a quatre ans	
Alexandre a un an	
Roseline a cinq ans	
Anne a neuf ans	
Martine a trois ans	

6. For each pair of people write who is the oldest, as shown in the example

A	B	OLDER
J'ai onze ans	J'ai treize ans	B
J'ai trois ans	J'ai seize ans	
J'ai deux ans	J'ai douze ans	
J'ai quinze ans	J'ai treize ans	
J'ai quatorze ans	J'ai onze ans	
J'ai huit ans	J'ai neuf ans	
J'ai onze ans	J'ai sept ans	

Unit 1. Talking about my age: READING

Je m'appelle Nico. Je suis argentin. J'ai douze ans et j'habite à Buenos Aires, la capitale de l'Argentine. J'ai un frère qui s'appelle Antonio. Antonio a quatorze ans. Ma sœur s'appelle Amélie et elle a sept ans.

Je m'appelle Ramon. Je suis espagnol. J'ai dix ans et j'habite à Madrid, la capitale de l'Espagne. J'ai une sœur qui s'appelle Barbara et un frère qui s'appelle Paco. Barbara a cinq ans. Paco a neuf ans.

Je m'appelle Marco. Je suis italien. J'ai treize ans et j'habite à Rome, la capitale de l'Italie. J'ai un frère qui s'appelle Robbie. Robbie a quinze ans. J'ai aussi une petite sœur, elle s'appelle Léa et elle a dix ans.

Je m'appelle Marine. Je suis française. J'ai dix ans et j'habite à Paris, la capitale de la France. J'ai une sœur qui s'appelle Fabienne. Fabienne a onze ans. J'ai aussi un frère qui s'appelle Pierre. Pierre a huit ans.

1. Find the French for the following items in Nico's text

a. I am Argentinian

b. My name is

c. The capital

d. In Buenos Aires

e. Who is called Antonio

f. I am twelve

g. Fourteen

2. Answer the following questions about Ramon

a. Where is Ramon from?

b. How old is he?

c. How many siblings does he have?

d. What are their names and ages?

Je m'appelle Hans. Je suis allemand. J'ai quatorze ans et j'habite à Berlin en Allemagne. J'ai deux frères. Mon frère aîné s'appelle Patrick et mon frère cadet s'appelle Norbert. Patrick a seize ans et Norbert a quinze ans.

3. Complete the table below

	Age	Nationality	How many siblings	Ages of siblings
Marco				
Nico				
Ramon				

Je m'appelle Kaori. Je suis japonaise. J'ai sept ans et j'habite à Tokyo, la capitale du Japon. J'ai une sœur qui s'appelle Yoko. Yoko a treize ans. J'ai aussi un frère qui s'appelle Hiroto. Hiroto a dix ans.

4. Hans, Kaori or Marine?

a. Who is from Germany?

b. Who has an 11 year old sister?

c. Who is 11 years old?

d. Who has an older brother aged 16?

e. Who has a 15 year old brother?

Unit 1. Talking about my age: TRANSLATION

1. Faulty translation: spot and correct (in the English) any translation mistakes you find below

a. Je m'appelle Patricia: *Her name is Patricia*

b. J'ai deux sœurs: *I have two brothers*

c. Ma sœur s'appelle Martine:
My mother is called Martine

d. Mon frère a cinq ans: *My sister is 5*

e. J'ai quinze ans: *I am five*

f. Mon frère a huit ans: *My brother is seven*

g. Je n'ai pas de frère: *I don't have a sister*

h. J'ai seize ans: *I am 17*

i. J'ai douze ans: *I am 13*

j. Il s'appelle Jean: *My name is Jean*

2. French to English translation

a. Mon frère s'appelle Jean.

b. J'ai quinze ans.

c. Mon frère a six ans.

d. Ma sœur s'appelle Mariana.

e. J'ai sept ans.

f. J'habite à Paris.

g. Ma sœur a quatorze ans.

h. J'ai un frère et une sœur.

i. Marie a douze ans.

j. Anne a neuf ans.

3. English to French translation

a. My name is Paul. I am six.

b. My brother is fifteen years old.

c. I am twelve.

d. My sister is called Anne.

e. I am fourteen.

f. I have a brother and a sister.

g. My name is Philippe and I am fourteen.

h. My name is Gabriel and I am eleven.

i. My name is Cédric. I am ten. I have a brother and a sister.

j. My sister is called Léa. She is twelve.

k. I am thirteen.

l. My brother is called Tanguy and he is sixteen.

m. My name is Pierre and I have two sisters.

Unit 1. Talking about my age: WRITING

1. Complete the words

a. J___ m'a_____ Paul.

b. J'_____ quato_____ a_____.

c. __ai un__ s_____r.

d. M___ f_____ s' a_____e Julien.

e. Je m'_____lle Patrice.

f. Mon _____ère s'_____lle Denis.

g. ___ai tr_____e ans.

h. Ma s_____r s'_____Anne.

2. Write out the numbers in French

Nine: N_____

Seven: S_____

Twelve: D_____

Five: C_____

Fourteen: Q_____

Sixteen: S_____

Thirteen: T_____

Four: Q_____

3. Spot and correct the spelling mistakes

a. Je m'appele Paul.

b. J'ai treze ans.

c. Mon frère à cinq ans.

d. Ma sir s'appelle Marie.

e. J'ai m'appelle Patrice.

f. Ma sœur s'appeller Alexandra.

4. Complete with a suitable word

a. Ma sœur s'_____ Laura.

b. _____ frère a quinze ans.

c. Je _____ Marc.

d. J'ai un _____ qui s'appelle Philippe.

e. J'ai une _____ qui s'appelle Anne.

f. Mon frère ____ quatorze ans.

5. Guided writing: write 4 short paragraphs in the first person singular 'I' each describing the people below

	Age	Lives in	Nationality	Brother's name and age	Sister's name and age
Samuel	12	Buenos Aires	Argentinian	Gonzalo 9	Anna 8
Rebeca	15	Madrid	Spanish	Jaime 13	Valentina 5
Michael	11	Berlin	German	Thomas 7	Gerda 12
Kyoko	10	Osaka	Japanese	Ken 6	Rena 1

6. Describe this person in the third person:

Name: Georges
Age: 12
Lives in: Toulouse
Brother: Marc, 13 years old
Sister: Sophie, 15 years old

THE LANGUAGE GYM

UNIT 2
Saying when our birthday is

In this unit you will learn to say:

- Where you and another person (e.g. a friend) are from
- When your birthday is
- Numbers from 15 to 31
- Months
- I am / He is / She is
- Names of French speaking locations
- Where you live

UNIT 2
Saying when my birthday is

Je m'appelle Julien *I am called Julien*	**je suis de Paris** *I am from Paris* ***j'ai X ans** *I am X years old*	**et** *and*	**mon anniversaire est le** *my birthday is the*	1 premier *first* 2 deux 3 trois 4 quatre 5 cinq 6 six 7 sept 8 huit 9 neuf 10 dix 11 onze 12 douze 13 treize 14 quatorze 15 quinze 16 seize 17 dix-sept 18 dix-huit 19 dix-neuf 20 vingt 21 vingt-et-un 22 vingt-deux 23 vingt-trois 24 vingt-quatre 25 vingt-cinq 26 vingt-six 27 vingt-sept 28 vingt-huit 29 vingt-neuf 30 trente 31 trente-et-un	**janvier** *January* **février** **mars** **avril** **mai** **juin** **juillet** **août** **septembre** **octobre** **novembre** **décembre**
Mon amie s'appelle Catherine *My friend is called Catherine* **Mon ami s'appelle Francis** *My friend is called Francis*	**il/elle est de Biarritz** *he/she is from Biarritz* ***il/elle a X ans** *he/she is X years old*		**son anniversaire est le** *his/her birthday is the*		

AUTHOR'S NOTE: *J'ai or il/elle a actually means "I have" and "he/she has" in French. You use this verb for telling age. You will see it many times throughout this booklet! ☺

Unit 2. Saying when my birthday is: VOCABULARY BUILDING

1. Complete with the missing word

a. Je _____ Gustave. *My name is Gustave.*

b. Mon _____ s'appelle Marie.
My friend is called Marie.

c. _____ ami s'appelle Julien. *My friend is called Julien.*

d. Mon _____ est le…
My birthday is on the…

e. Le _____ mai. *The fifth of May.*

f. Le _____ novembre.
The 18th November.

g. Le quatre _____. *The 4th July.*

h. _____ anniversaire est le… *His/her birthday is on…*

2. Match up

Avril	May
Novembre	My birthday
Décembre	My friend (f)
Mai	April
Janvier	November
Février	He/she is called
Mon anniversaire	December
Mon ami	I am called
Mon amie	February
Je m'appelle	January
Il/elle s'appelle	My friend (m)
Août	August

3. Translate into English

a. Le quatorze janvier:

b. Le huit mai:

c. Le sept février:

d. Le vingt mars:

e. Le dix-neuf août:

f. Le vingt-cinq juillet:

g. Le vingt-quatre septembre:

h. Le quinze avril:

4. Add the missing letter

a. ann__versaire   c. ma__s   e. a__ril   g. j__nvier   i. ju__llet   k. d__cembre

b. fé__rier   d. m__i   f. jui__   h. ao__t   j. novem__re   l. se__tembre

5. Broken words

a. L___ t_____ j_____: *The 3ʳᵈ of Jan*

b. L___ c_____ j_____: *The 5ᵗʰ of July*

c. L___ n_____ a_____: *The 9ᵗʰ of Aug*

d. L___ d_____ m_____: *The 12ᵗʰ of March*

e. L___ s_____ a_____: *The 16ᵗʰ of April*

f. L___ d_____ d_____:
The 19ᵗʰ of Dec

g. L___ v_____ o_____: *The 20ᵗʰ of Oct*

h. L___ v_____ m_____:
The 24ᵗʰ of May

i. L___ t_____ s_____: *The 30ᵗʰ of Sept*

6. Complete with a suitable word

a. Je _____ Ronan.

b. Mon _____ est le onze mai.

c. J'ai neuf _____.

d. Mon _____ s'appelle Gian.

e. Gian _____ dix ans.

f. Son _____ est le trois juin.

g. Mon _____ est le dix-huit
juillet.

h. Mon ami ____ appelle Dylan.

i. _____ anniversaire est le quatre août.

j. Le huit n_____.

k. ____ m'appelle Gustave Eiffel.

Unit 2. Saying when my birthday is: READING

Je m'appelle Rodrigue. J'ai douze ans et j'habite en Martinique. Mon anniversaire est le douze septembre. Mon amie s'appelle Gabrielle et elle a quatorze ans. Son anniversaire est le vingt-huit mai. Pendant mon temps libre, je joue toujours de la guitare. Gabrielle aussi!

Mon autre amie s'appelle Carla. Elle a trente-cinq ans et elle est professeure. Son anniversaire est le vingt-et-un juin. Carla a un frère aîné. Son anniversaire est le huit janvier.

Je m'appelle Serge. J'ai vingt-deux ans et j'habite à Sospel, dans le sud-est de la France. Mon anniversaire est le dix septembre. Mon amie s'appelle Irène et elle a quinze ans. Son anniversaire est le vingt-huit mai. Pendant mon temps libre je regarde toujours la télé.

Je m'appelle Mélanie. J'ai sept ans et j'habite à Saint-Denis, la capitale de la Réunion. Mon anniversaire est le cinq décembre. J'ai deux frères, Jules et Éric. Jules a onze ans et il est très sympa. Son anniversaire est le trente septembre. Éric est très pénible. Il a treize ans et son anniversaire est le cinq janvier.

Je m'appelle Anthony. J'ai huit ans et je vis à Saint-Tropez sur la Côte d'Azur, dans le sud de la France. Mon anniversaire est le neuf août. Ma petite sœur s'appelle Sandra et elle a quatre ans. Elle est très amicale. Son anniversaire est le neuf août. Comme moi!

Mon ami s'appelle Victor et il a dix-sept ans. Son anniversaire est le vingt-cinq octobre.

1. Find the French for the following items in Rodrigue's text

a. I am called:

b. I am 12 years old:

c. I live in Martinique:

d. My birthday is:

e. The twelfth:

f. Her birthday is:

g. In my free time:

h. My friend:

i. Is called:

j. She is 35:

k. The 21st of June:

l. Has an older brother:

m. The eighth of January:

3. Answer the following questions about Mélanie's text

a. How old is she?

b. Where is Saint-Denis?

c. When is her birthday?

d. How many brothers does she have?

e. Which brother is nice?

f. How old in Éric?

g. When is his birthday?

2. Complete with the missing words

Je m'appelle Anne. _____ treize _____ et je _____ à Paris, ___ France.

Mon _____ est le vingt-neuf décembre. Mon frère _____ neuf _____ et son anniversaire est le _____(1st) avril.

4. Find Someone Who

a. …has a birthday in December

b. …is 22 years old

c. …shares a birthday with a sibling

d. …likes to play guitar with their friend

e. …has a friend who is 35 years old

f. …has a birthday in late September

g. …has a little sister

h. …has one good and one bad sibling

i. …is from the southeast of France

THE LANGUAGE GYM

Unit 2. Saying when my birthday is: WRITING

1. Complete with the missing letters

a. Je m'appel_ _ Paul.

b. Je su_s d_ Brest.

c. M_n anniversai_ _, c'est le quin_ _ ju_n.

d. J'_ _ quat_ _ze a_s.

e. Mon ami_ s' appell_ Catherine.

f. Catherine e_t de Marseille.

g. Mon am_ Michel es_ d_ Saint-Étienne.

h. Michel a onz_ a_ s.

2. Spot and correct the spelling and grammar mistakes

a. Mon anniversary, c'est le quatre janvier.

b. J'ai m'appelle Paul.

c. Je suis de le Brest.

d. Mon amie se appelle Catherine.

e. Catherine as onze ans.

f. J'ai quatorce ans.

g. Ma anniversaire, c'est le quatre mars.

h. J'ai kinze ans.

i. Je m'apple Denis.

3. Answer the questions in French

Comment tu t'appelles?

Quel âge as-tu?

Quelle est la date de ton anniversaire?

Comment s'appelle ton frère/ta sœur?

Quel âge a ton frère/ta sœur?

Quelle est la date de son anniversaire?

4. Write out the dates below in words as shown in the example

a. 15.05: le quinze mai

b. 10.06:

c. 20.03:

d. 19.02:

e. 25.12:

f. 01.01:

g. 22.11:

h. 11.02:

5. Guided writing: write 4 short paragraphs in the 1st person singular 'I' describing the people below

Name	Town/ City	Age	Birthday	Name of brother	Brother's birthday
Samuel	Sospel	11	25.12	Jules	19.02
Alex	Bordeaux	14	21.07	Philippe	21.04
André	Grasse	12	01.01	Julien	20.06
Charles	Morzine	16	02.11	Michel	12.10

6. Describe this person in the third person:

Name: Jean-Marc

Age: 12

Lives in: Albertville

Birthday: 21.06

Brother: Jean, 16 years old

Birthday: 01.12

Unit 2. Saying when my birthday is: TRANSLATION

1. Faulty translation: spot and correct (in the English) any mistakes you find below

a. Mon anniversaire est le vingt-huit avril: *His birthday is on the 27th April*

b. Je m'appelle Candide et je suis de France: *Your name is Candide and you are from France*

c. J'ai vingt-trois ans: *I am 22 years old*

d. Mon ami s'appelle Jean: *My friend I am called Jean*

e. Il a vingt-six ans: *I have 26 years old*

f. Son anniversaire est le quatre avril: *My birthday is the 14th April*

3. Phrase-level translation

a. My name is Anne:

b. I am ten years old:

c. My birthday is the 12th June:

d. The seventh of May:

e. My friend is called Béatrice:

f. She is twelve years old:

g. Her birthday is the…

h. The 23rd of August:

i. The 29th April:

Author's note: go back to e. Did you make Béatrice a girl? "amie" Well done if you did! ☺

2. From French to English

a. Le dix-huit octobre:

b. Mon anniversaire est le…

c. Mon ami s'appelle…

d. Son anniversaire est le…

e. Le onze janvier:

f. Le quatorze février:

g. Le vingt-cinq décembre:

h. Le huit juillet:

i. Le premier juin:

4. Sentence-level translation

a. My name is Claude. I am 30 years old. I live in France. My birthday is on the 11th March.

b. My brother is called Pierre. He is 14 years old. His birthday is on the 18th August.

c. My friend is called Jean. He is 22 years old and his birthday is on the 14th January.

d. My friend is called Anne. She is 18 years old and her birthday is on the 25th July.

e. My friend is called Anthony. He is 20 years old. His birthday is on the 24th September.

UNIT 3
Describing hair and eyes

In this unit you will learn:
- To describe what a person's hair and eyes are like
- To describe details about their faces (e.g. beard and glasses)
- Colours
- I wear / He wears / She wears

You will also revisit:
- Common French names
- The verb "avoir" in the first and third person singular
- Numbers from 1 to 15

UNIT 3
Describing hair and eyes

Je m'appelle... *I am called* **Il/elle s'appelle** *He/she is called*	**Anthony** **Charles** **Pierre** **Émilie** **Isabelle** **Marie** **Jules** **Julien** **Robert**	**et** *and*	**j'ai** *I have* **il/elle a** *he/she has*	**six ans** *6 years* **sept ans** *7 years* **huit ans** *8 years* **neuf ans** *9 years* **dix ans** *10 years* **onze ans** *11 years* **douze ans** *12 years* **treize ans** *13 years* **quatorze ans** *14 years* **quinze ans** *15 years*
J'ai les cheveux *I have...hair* **Il/elle a les cheveux** *he/she has...hair*	**blonds** *blond* **bruns** *brown* **châtains** *light brown* **noirs** *black* **roux** *red*	**et**	**courts** *short* **en épis** *spiky* **frisés** *curly* **longs** *long* **mi-longs** *mid-length* **ondulés** *wavy* **raides** *straight* **rasés** *shaved*	
J'ai les yeux *I have... eyes* **Il/elle a les yeux** *he/she has... eyes*	**bleus** *blue* **marron** *brown* **noirs** *black* **verts** *green*	**et**	**je porte** *I wear* **il/elle porte** *he/she wears*	**des lunettes** *glasses*
			j'ai *I have* **il a** *he has*	**une moustache** *a moustache* **une barbe** *a beard*

Author's note: in the negative form in French the "des" or "une" turns into "de"
Examples: -Je **ne** porte **pas de** lunettes. *I don't wear glasses.*
         -Je **n'ai pas de** moustache/barbe. *I don't have a moustache/beard.*
         -Elle **ne** porte **pas de** lunettes. *She doesn't wear glasses.*
         -Il **n'a pas de** moustache/barbe. *He doesn't have a moustache/beard.*

Unit 3. Describing hair and eyes: VOCABULARY BUILDING

1. Complete with the missing word

a. J'ai les cheveux c_____
I have light brown hair

b. J'ai les cheveux b_____ *I have blond hair*

c. J'ai une _____ *I have a beard*

d. J'ai les yeux _____ *I have blue eyes*

e. Je porte des _____ *I wear glasses*

f. J'ai les cheveux m_____
I have mid-length hair

g. J'ai les yeux n_____ *I have black eyes*

h. J'ai les cheveux r_____ *I have red hair*

2. Match up

Les cheveux châtains	Blue eyes
Les cheveux noirs	Light brown hair
Les cheveux blonds	Black eyes
Les yeux noirs	A moustache
Les lunettes	Green eyes
Une moustache	Black hair
Les yeux bleus	Short hair
Les yeux verts	Long hair
Les cheveux courts	Red hair
Les cheveux longs	Blond hair
Les cheveux roux	Glasses

3. Translate into English

a. Les cheveux frisés:

b. Les yeux bleus:

c. Je porte des lunettes:

d. Les cheveux blonds:

e. Les yeux verts:

f. Les cheveux roux:

g. Les yeux noirs:

h. Les cheveux noirs:

4. Add the missing letter

a. lo__g   c. __heveux   e. ble_   g. fris__s   i. no__r   k. yeu__

b. lu__ettes d. ba__be   f. en__pis   h. __aides   j. m__-longs   l. je p__rte

5. Broken words

a. J'___ le__ c_____ f_____: *I have curly hair*

b. Je _____ d___ l_____: *I wear glasses*

c. __ai les c_____ c_____: *I have short hair*

d. Je n'___ p___ de m_____:
I don't have a moustache

e. J'___ ___s y_____ marron: *I have brown eyes*

f. __ai u___ b_____: *I have a beard*

g. J'ai h_____ a____: *I am eight years old*

h. J__ m'_____ M_____: *My name is Marie*

i. J'___ n_____ a_____: *I am nine years old*

6. Complete with a suitable word

a. J'ai dix ____.

b. J'ai ____ barbe.

c. Je m'_____ Anthony.

d. J'ai _____ ans.

e. J'ai les cheveux _____.

f. Je porte des _____.

g. J'ai les _____ marron.

h. J'ai _____ cheveux noirs.

i. Je n'ai _____ de moustache.

j. _____ les cheveux longs.

k. _____ m'appelle Pierre.

l. J'ai quinze _____.

m. J'ai les yeux _____.

Unit 3. Describing hair and eyes: READING

Je m'appelle Martine. J'ai douze ans et j'habite à Fort-de-France, la capitale de la Martinique. J'ai les cheveux noirs, raides et courts et les yeux bleus. Je porte des lunettes. Mon anniversaire est le dix septembre. Ma sœur a les cheveux raides. Elle a dix ans.

Je m'appelle Irène. J'ai quinze ans et je vis à Libreville, la capitale du Gabon.
J'ai les cheveux roux, ondulés et longs et les yeux bleus. Je ne porte pas de lunettes. Mon anniversaire est le quinze décembre.

Je m'appelle Alexandre. J'ai neuf ans et j'habite à Ajaccio, la capitale de la Corse.
J'ai les cheveux mi-longs, châtains et ondulés et les yeux marron.
Je ne porte pas de lunettes. Mon anniversaire est le cinq décembre.

Mon frère s'appelle Tristan. Il a quinze ans. Il a les cheveux roux, longs et raides et les yeux verts.
Il porte des lunettes. Son anniversaire est le treize novembre. Il est très musclé.

Je m'appelle Céline. J'ai huit ans et je vis à Rabat, la capitale du Maroc. J'ai les cheveux châtains, longs et frisés et les yeux bleus. Je porte des lunettes. Mon anniversaire est le neuf mai. Chez moi, j'ai trois animaux: un cheval, un chien et un chat.

Mon frère s'appelle Serge. Il a quatorze ans. Il a les cheveux blonds, longs et raides et les yeux bleus comme moi. Il porte aussi des lunettes comme mon père. Son anniversaire est le deux juin. Il est très intelligent.

Je m'appelle Paul. J'ai dix ans et je vis à Paris, la capitale de la France. J'ai les cheveux blonds, raides et courts et les yeux verts. Je porte des lunettes. Mon anniversaire est le huit avril.

1. Find the French for the following items in Martine's text

a. I am called:

b. In:

c. I wear glasses:

d. My birthday is:

e. The tenth:

f. I have:

g. Straight:

h. Black:

i. Eyes:

2. Answer the following questions about Irène's text

a. How old is she?

b. Where is Libreville?

c. What colour is her hair?

d. Is her hair wavy, straight or curly?

e. What length is her hair?

f. What colour are her eyes?

g. When is her birthday?

3. Complete with the missing words

Je m'appelle Pierre. _____ dix ans et j'_____ à Dakar, la _____ du Sénégal. J'ai les _____ blonds, raides et courts et les _____ verts.
Je _____ des lunettes. Mon anniversaire ____ le huit avril.

4. Find Someone Who: answer the questions below about all 5 texts

a. Who has a brother called Serge?

b. Who is eight years old?

c. Who celebrates their birthday on the 9th May?

d. How many people wear glasses?

e. Who has red hair and blue eyes?

f. Who has a very intelligent brother?

g. Whose birthday is in April?

h. Who has brown, wavy hair and brown eyes?

Unit 3. Describing hair and eyes: TRANSLATION

1. Faulty translation: spot and correct (in the English) any translation mistakes you find below

a. J'ai les cheveux blonds: I have black eyes

b. Elle a les yeux bleus: he has brown eyes

c. J'ai une barbe: He has a beard

d. Il s'appelle Pierre: I am called Pierre

e. Il a les cheveux rasés: I have long hair

f. J'ai les yeux verts: I have blue eyes

g. J'habite à Paris: I am from Paris

2. From French to English

a. J'ai les cheveux blonds:

b. J'ai les yeux noirs:

c. Il a les cheveux raides:

d. Il porte des lunettes et il a une barbe:

e. J'ai une moustache:

f. Je porte des lunettes de soleil:

g. Je n'ai pas de barbe:

h. J'ai les cheveux frisés:

i. J'ai les cheveux longs:

3. Phrase-level translation

a. 'The' blond hair:

b. I am called:

c. I have:

d. 'The' blue eyes:

e. 'The' straight hair:

f. He has:

g. Ten years:

h. I have black eyes:

i. I have nine years:

j. 'The' brown eyes:

k. 'The' black hair:

l. She has:

4. Sentence-level translation

a. My name is Marc. I am ten years old. I have black and curly hair and blue eyes.

b. I am twelve years old. I have green eyes and blond, straight hair.

c. I am called Anne. I live in Marseille. I have long blond hair and brown eyes.

d. My name is Pierre. I live in Lyon. I have black hair, very short and wavy.

e. I am fifteen years old. I have black, curly long hair and green eyes.

f. I am thirteen years old. I have red, straight long hair and brown eyes.

Unit 3. Describing hair and eyes: WRITING

1. Split sentences

J'ai les cheveux	les yeux verts
J'ai une	barbe
J'ai	blonds
J'ai les	et frisés
J'ai les cheveux noirs	cheveux noirs
Je m'appelle	ans
J'ai dix	Martine

2. Rewrite the sentences in the correct order

a. cheveux les j'ai frisés

b. pas je barbe n'ai de

c. m'appelle je Richard

d. cheveux j'ai roux les

e. s' frère appelle Paul mon

3. Spot and correct the grammar and spelling errors

a. J'ai les yeu noirs   f. J'ai les raides cheveux

b. Mon frère m'appellent Anthony g. J'ai le yeux verts

c. Elle a cheveux frisés   h. J'ai des barbes

d. Elle appelle Martine   i. Je porte une lunette

e. J'ai quatorze an   j. Je n'ai pas moustache

4. Anagrams

a. xeyu = yeux

b. rbabe =

c. roins =

d. san =

e. suelb =

f. xour =

g. éssfri =

h. rtsev =

5. Guided writing – write 3 short paragraphs in the first person singular 'I' describing the people below

Name	Age	Hair	Eyes	Glasses	Beard	Moustache
Louis	12	brown curly long	green	wears	does not have	has
Anne	11	blond straight short	blue	doesn't wear	does not have	does not have
Alex	10	red wavy mid-length	black	wears	has	does not have

6. Describe this person in the third person:

Name: Georges
Age: 15
Hair: black, curly, very short
Eyes: brown
Glasses: no
Beard: yes

UNIT 4
Saying where I live and am from

In this unit you will learn to talk about:

- Where you live and are from
- If you live in an apartment or a house
- What your accommodation looks like
- Where it is located
- The names of renowned cities and countries in the French speaking world
- The verb 'Être' (to be)

You will also revisit:

- Introducing yourself
- Telling age and birthday

UNIT 4
Saying where I live and am from

Je m'appelle David et... *my name is David and...*	je vis dans *I live in* j'habite dans *I live in*	une *a*	**belle** *beautiful* **grande** *big* **jolie** *pretty* **petite** *small*	**maison** *house*	**dans le centre** *in the centre*
		un appartement *a flat*	**dans un bâtiment ancien** *in an old building* **dans un bâtiment moderne** *in a modern building* **dans un bâtiment neuf** *in a new building*		**dans la banlieue** *on the outskirts* **sur la côte** *on the coast*
	je suis de *I am from*	Biarritz	**dans le Pays basque** *southwest region of France*		
		Brest	**en Bretagne (en France)** *northwest of France*		
		Bruxelles	**en Belgique (la capitale)** *capital of Belgium*		
		Casablanca	**au Maroc (sur la côte)** *coast of Morocco*		
		Dakar	**au Sénégal (la capitale)** *capital of Senegal*		
		Fort-de-France	**en Martinique (la capitale)** *capital of Martinique*		
		Libreville	**au Gabon (la capitale)** *capital of Gabon*		
		Montréal	**au Québec** *Quebec, Canadian province*		
		Nice	**en Provence (en France)** *southeast of France*		
		Nouméa	**en Nouvelle Calédonie** *New Caledonia*		
		Paris	**en France (la capitale)** *capital of France*		
		Saint-Denis	**à la Réunion (la capitale)** *capital of Reunion Island*		
		Strasbourg	**en Alsace (en France)** *northeast region of France*		

Unit 4. Saying where I live and am from: VOCABULARY BUILDING

1. Complete with the missing words

a. J'habite dans _____ jolie maison. *I live in a pretty house.*

b. J'aime mon _____. *I like my flat.*

c. Je suis _____ Paris. *I am from Paris.*

d. _____ dans une petite maison. *I live in a small house.*

e. Un appartement dans un _____ ancien.
A flat in an old building.

f. _____ de Saint-Martin, dans les Caraïbes.
I am from Saint-Martin, in the Caribbean.

g. J'habite dans une très _____ maison.
I live in a very small house.

2. Match up

Le centre	Big
Jolie	Small
Grande	Old
Bâtiment	Pretty
Ancien	The centre
La banlieue	The coast
La côte	I am from
Maroc	The outskirts
Je suis de	Beautiful
Belle	I live in
Petite	Morocco
J'habite dans	Building

3. Translate into English

a. Je suis de Bordeaux:

b. J'habite dans une maison:

c. Mon appartement est petit:

d. Je suis de Nice, en Provence:

e. Dans un bâtiment moderne:

f. Je suis de Rabat, la capitale du Maroc:

g. J'habite dans un appartement sur la côte:

h. Je suis de Nantes, en France:

4. Add the missing letter(s)

a. Casa__lanca   c. B__est   e. M__ntréal   g. Bru__elles   i. S__rasbourg

b. Pari__   d. Lib__eville f. Nou__éa   h. Biarrit_   j. F__rt-de-F__ance

5. Broken words

a. Je s___ d__ B_____ d____, l_ P___ b_____.
I am from Biarritz, in the Basque country.

b. Je v__ d____ u_ g_____ m_____.
I live in a big house.

c. J_ s____ d__ P_____, l_ c_____ d__ l__
F_____.
I am from Paris, the capital of France.

d. J'_____ d___ u_ a_____ s___ l_ c____ e__
B_____.
I live in a flat on the coast in Brittany.

e. Je v__ d____ u___ p_____, mais j_____
m_____.
I live in a small but pretty house.

f. Je s_____ d__ B_____ et j'_____ d____
u__ b_____ a_____.
I am from Brussels and I live in an old building.

6. Complete with a suitable word

a. Je suis _____ Brest.

b. Je vis _____ une jolie maison.

c. Dans un _____ ancien.

d. J'habite dans une maison dans la _____.

e. Saint-Denis est la capitale de la _____.

f. Je vis dans une _____ maison.

g. Je suis de _____.

h. J'habite dans un appartement dans un bâtiment _____.

Unit 4. "Geography test": Using your own knowledge (and a bit of help from Google/your teacher) match the numbers to the cities

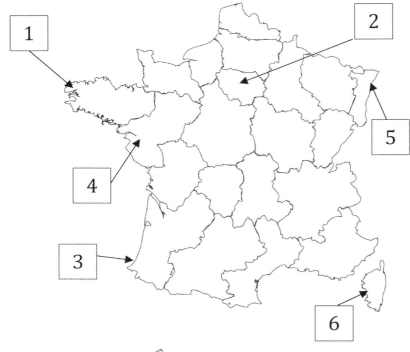

France	
Num	**City**
	Ajaccio
	Biarritz
	Brest
	Nantes
	Paris
	Strasbourg

Africa	
Num	**City**
	Antananarivo (Madagascar)
	Bamako (Mali)
	Brazzaville (Congo)
	Casablanca (Morocco)
	Dakar (Sénégal)
	Libreville (Gabon)
	Niamey (Niger)
	Ouagadougou (Burkina Faso)
	Yamoussoukro (côte d'ivoire)

Unit 4. Saying where I live and am from: READING

Je m'appelle Charles. J'ai vingt-deux ans et mon anniversaire est le neuf août. Je vis à Biarritz au Pays basque. Je vis dans une jolie maison dans le centre-ville.

J'ai deux frères, Édouard et Renaud. J'aime beaucoup Édouard, mais Renaud est très stupide.

Mon ami Julien habite à Brest, dans le nord-ouest de la France. Il habite dans un appartement dans un bâtiment ancien, aussi en centre-ville.

Je m'appelle Isabelle. J'ai vingt-et-un ans et je vis à Dakar, la capitale du Sénégal avec mon amie Marina. Nous habitons dans un grand appartement moderne dans la banlieue. Mon anniversaire est le deux juin et l'anniversaire de Marina est le 12 juillet.

Dans mon appartement, j'ai un chien qui s'appelle 'Bandit'. Il est très grand et marrant. Son anniversaire est le premier avril. Bandit a trois ans. J'ai aussi une araignée, jolie et très grande, qui s'appelle Pépette. L'anniversaire de mon araignée est aussi le premier avril. Donc je fais une fête pour mes deux animaux en même temps. C'est très pratique.

Je m'appelle Raymond. J'ai quinze ans et j'habite à Ajaccio, la capitale de la Corse. Dans ma famille, nous sommes quatre personnes: mes parents, mon frère, Guillaume, et moi. Mon anniversaire est le onze septembre et Guillaume aussi. Nous sommes jumeaux!

Je m'appelle Stéphanie. J'ai neuf ans et je vis à Casablanca, sur la côte du Maroc. J'habite dans une maison avec ma famille: mes parents et ma grande sœur, Sarah. Mon anniversaire est le neuf mai et l'anniversaire de Sarah est le trente mars. Elle a onze ans. Ma maison est grande et jolie et elle est au bord de la mer. Je l'aime beaucoup!

1. Find the French for the following in Isabelle's text

a. My name is

b. I am 21 years old

c. I live in…

d. A big flat

e. On the outskirts

f. The 2nd of june

g. I have a dog

h. He is very big

i. His birthday is on the 1st April

j. He is 3 years old

k. I also have a spider

2. Complete the statements below based on Charles' text

a. I am _____ years old.

b. My birthday is the _____ of _____.

c. I live in a _____ house.

d. My house is in the _____ of town.

e. I like Édouard, but Renaud is _____.

f. My friend Julien _____ in Brest.

g. He lives in an old _____.

3. Answer the questions on the four texts above

a. How old is Raymond?

b. Why do Raymond and Guillaume have the same birthday? *(What do you think a 'jumeau' is?)*

c. Who only likes one of his siblings?

d. Who has two pets that share a birthday?

e. Why is it convenient that they share a birthday?

f. Who has a friend that lives in a different city?

g. Who lives with their really good friend?

h. Who does not live in France?

i. Whose birthday is on the twelfth of July?

4. Correct any of the statements below about Stéphanie's text which are incorrect

a. Stéphanie habite à Casablanca, dans le centre du Maroc.

b. Dans la famille de Stéphanie, il y a *(there are)* quatre personnes.

c. Son anniversaire est en mars.

d. L'anniversaire de Sarah est le trois mars.

e. Stéphanie habite dans une petite maison sur la côte.

f. Elle aime beaucoup sa maison.

Unit 4. Saying where I live and am from: TRANSLATION/WRITING

1. Translate into English

a. J'habite dans:

b. Une maison:

c. Un appartement:

d. Joli:

e. Grand:

f. Dans un bâtiment:

g. Ancien:

h. Moderne:

i. Dans le centre:

j. Dans la banlieue:

k. Sur la côte:

l. Je suis de:

m. En France:

n. Au Maroc:

o. En Nouvelle Calédonie:

2. Gapped sentences

a. J'habite dans une belle _____: *I live in a beautiful house*

b. Un appartement dans un _____ neuf:
A flat in a new building

c. J'habite dans un petit _____: *I live in a small flat*

d. Une _____ dans la _____: *A house on the outskirts*

e. __ ____ __ Paris, la capitale de la France:
I am from Paris, the capital of France

3. Complete the sentences with a suitable word

a. J'habite à _____ , la capitale du Sénégal.

b. Je suis de Nice , en _____.

c. Je vis dans un _____ appartement dans la _____.

d. J'habite dans une jolie maison dans le _____.

e. Je _____ de Bruxelles, la _____ de la Belgique.

f. Je vis dans un _____ moderne dans le centre.

4. Phrase-level translation En to Fr

a. I live in…

b. I am from…

c. A house…

d. A flat…

e. New (m)…

f. Small (m)…

g. In an old building…

h. In the centre…

i. On the outskirts…

j. On the coast…

k. In the Basque country…

5. Sentence-level translation En to Fr

a. I am from Biarritz, in the Basque country in France. I live in a big and pretty house on the outskirts.

b. I am from Montréal in Québec. I live in a small and pretty flat in the centre.

c. I am from Saint-Denis, the capital of Reunion Island. I live in a flat in a new building on the coast. My flat is small, but beautiful.

d. I am from Casablanca, in Morocco. I live in a flat in an old building on the outskirts. I like my flat.

Unit 4. Saying where I live and am from: WRITING

1. Complete with the missing letters

a. Je m'appel_ _ Paul.

b. Je v_ _ dans une jo_ _e mai_o_.

c. J_ v_s dans un gran_ a_ _artement.

d. J'h_ _ite dans une _ _ison dans le cent_ _.

e. Je s_ _s de Bre_ _ en Breta_ _e.

f. Je _ui_ de Bru_elle_ en Belgi_ue.

g. Je v_ _ dans un pe_ _t appartemen_ dans la banlie_ _.

h. _e suis de Libre _ _ _ _ _ au Ga_ _ _.

2. Spot and correct the spelling mistakes

a. Je suis de Best en Bretane.

b. Je vie à Biorritz dans le Pais basque.

c. J'habite dans une petit maison.

d. Je vis dans un grande appartement.

e. Je vis dans un moderne bâtiment.

f. Je vis en Nouveau Calédonie.

g. Je suis de Casanova au Maroc.

3. Answer the questions in French

a. Comment tu t'appelles?

b. Quel âge as-tu?

c. Quelle est la date de ton anniversaire?

d. D'où es-tu?

e. Où habites-tu?

f. Tu habites dans une maison ou un appartement?

4. Anagrams (regions of France and countries)

a. stBre = *Brest*

b. queBas =

c. bourgStras=

d. ébecuQ =

e. coMar =

f. taBregne=

g. ceNi =

h. vencePro =

i. ztirraiB =

j. iqueMartin =

5. Guided writing: write 5 short paragraphs in the 1st person singular 'I' describing the people below

Name	Age	Birthday	City	Country or region
Samuel	12	20.06	Biarritz	Pays basque
Alain	14	14.10	Paris	France
André	11	14.01	Brest	Bretagne
Charles	13	17.11	Dakar	Sénégal
Caroline	15	19.10	Nice	Provence

6. Describe this person in the third person:

Name: Alexandre

Age: 16

Birthday: 15th May

Country of origin: Montréal, Québec

Country of residence: Paris, France

THE LANGUAGE GYM

UNIT 5
Talking about my family members, saying their age and how well I get along with them. Counting to 100.

Revision quickie – Numbers 1-100/dates/birthdays

In this unit you will learn to talk about:

- How many people there are in your family and who they are
- If you get along with them
- Words for family members
- What their age is
- Numbers from 31 to 100

You will also revisit

- Numbers from 1 to 31
- Hair and eyes description

UNIT 5
Talking about my family members, saying their age and how well I get on with them. Counting to 100.

Dans ma famille, j'ai *In my family, I have…*	**mon cousin, Tanguy.** *my cousin, Tanguy.* **mon grand-père, Léon.** *my grandfather Léon.* **mon père, Jean.** *my father Jean.* **mon oncle, Yvan.** *my uncle Yvan.* **mon grand frère, Ronan.** *my big brother Ronan.* **mon petit frère, Olivier.** *my little brother Olivier.*	**Il a**	**un** *1*	**an**
Il y a quatre personnes dans ma famille *There are four people in my family…*			**deux** **trois** **quatre** **cinq** **six** **sept** **huit** **neuf** **dix** **onze** *11* **douze** *12* **treize** *13* **quatorze** *14* **quinze** *15* **seize** *16*	
Je m'entends bien avec… *I get on well with…* **Je ne m'entends pas bien…** *I don't get on well with…*	**ma cousine, Claire.** *my (girl) cousin Claire.* **ma grand-mère, Adeline.** *my grandmother Adeline.* **ma mère, Anne.** *my mother Anne.* **ma tante, Gisèle.** *my aunt Gisèle.* **ma grande sœur, Léa.** *my big sister Léa.* **ma petite sœur, Sophie.** *my little sister Sophie.*	**Elle a**	**dix-sept** *17* **dix-huit** *18* **dix-neuf** *19* **vingt** *20* **vingt-et-un** *21* **vingt-deux** *22* **trente** *30* **trente-et-un** *31* **trente deux** *32* **quarante** *40* **cinquante** *50* **soixante** *60* **soixante-dix** *70* **quatre-vingts** *80* **quatre-vingt-dix** *90* **cent** *100*	**ans**

Unit 5. Talking about my family + Counting to 100: VOCAB BUILDING

1. Complete with the missing word

a. Dans ma f_____ j'ai: *In my family I have*

b. Il y a _____ personnes: *There are five people*

c. Mon _____ , Claude:
My grandfather, Claude

d. Mon grand-père _____ quatre-vingts ans:
My grandfather is 80 years old

e. Ma _____ Éliane: *My mother Éliane*

f. Elle _____ cinquante ans:
She is 50 years old

2. Match up

Seize	12
Douze	48
Vingt-et-un	13
Dix	16
Trente-trois	10
Treize	21
Quarante-huit	15
Cinquante-deux	5
Cinq	33
Quinze	52

3. Translate into English

a. Je m'entends mal avec:

b. Ma grand-mère, Thérèse:

c. Mon oncle:

d. Il y a quatre personnes:

e. Dans ma famille:

f. Je m'entends bien avec:

g. Mon père:

h. Elle a vingt ans:

4. Add the missing letters

a. fa__ille   c. p__rsonnes   e.fr__re   g. m__re   i. je m'entend__   k. qu__nze

b. j'a_   d. grand-p__re   f. gr__nd   h. c__usin   j. b__en   l. di__

5. Broken words

a. Il __ a s___ p_____ d_____ m__
f_____: *There are 6 people in my family*

b. M__ s_____ a d_____ a____:
My sister is 12 years old

c. D_____ m__ fam_____ j'___: *In my family I have*

d. M___ c_____ s'_____ Sylvain:
My male cousin is called Sylvain

e. M___ p_____ a c_____-c_____ a____:
My father is 55 years old

f. J__ m'_____ m__ a____ m__ g_____
f_____: *I get on badly with my big brother*

6. Complete with a suitable word

a. Dans ma _____.

b. _____ trois personnes.

c. Ma _____ sœur.

d. Elle a quatorze ____

e. Ma _____, Gisèle a trente-cinq ans.

f. Je m'entends _____ avec mon père.

g. Il y a quatre _____ dans ma famille.

h. Je _____ bien avec ma grand-mère.

i. Je m'entends _____ avec mon oncle.

Unit 5. Talking about my family + Counting to 100: VOCABULARY DRILLS

1. Match up

Dans ma	There are
Famille	In my
Il y a	With
Sept	I get on well
Je m'entends bien	Family
Avec	Seven

2. Complete with the missing word

a. _____ cinq personnes: *There are five people*

b. Mon _____, Jean, a soixante ans: *My father, Jean, is 60*

c. Je _____ bien avec mon oncle: *I get along with my uncle*

d. Je m'entends _____ avec mon cousin:
I get along badly with my cousin

e. Ma tante, Gisèle, ___ quarante ans: *My aunt, Gisèle, is 40*

f. Il a _____ ans: *He is 18*

g. _____ a vingt-six ans: *She is 26*

h. Ma _____, Adèle, a quatre-vingts ans:
My grandma, Adèle is 80

3. Translate into English

a. Il a neuf ans:

b. Elle a quarante ans:

c. Mon père a quarante-quatre ans:

d. Je m'entends mal avec mon oncle:

e. Je m'entends bien avec mon frère:

f. Ma petite sœur a cinq ans:

g. Il y a huit personnes dans ma famille:

h. Dans ma famille il y a six personnes:

4. Complete with the missing letters

a. Mon g____d frère: *My big brother*

b. Dans ma fa____lle i___ ___ trois personnes:
In my family there are 3 people

c. Mon cousin a dix-____ ans: *My cousin is 18*

d. Je m'_____ds très m____ avec mon frère:
I get along very badly with my brother

e. Mon o____ a quar____e a__s:
My uncle is 40 years old

f. Je m'entends t____ bi___avec ma cousine:
I get along very well with my cousin

g. Mon co_____ a q____ze ans:
My cousin is 15 years old

h. Je m'entends assez bien avec e____:
I get along quite well with her

5. Translate into French

a. In my family:

b. There are:

c. My father:

d. Is 40 years old:

e. I get along well:

f. With:

6. Spot and correct the errors

a. Dans ma famille il y a trois personne.

b. Ma grand-père Adèle.

c. Mon frère as neuf ans.

d. Je m'entends mall avec mon cousin.

e. Mon cousin a hui ans.

f. Mon grande frère, David.

Unit 5. Talking about my family + Counting to 100: TRANSLATION

1. Match up

Vingt	30
Trente	70
Quarante	100
Cinquante	50
Soixante	20
Quatre-vingts	80
Quatre-vingt-dix	40
Cent	60
Soixante-dix	90

2. Write out in French

a. 35: trente-cinq

b. 63: s

c. 89: q

d. 74: s

e. 98: q

f. 100: c

g. 82: q

h. 24: v

i. 17: d

3. Write out with the missing number

a. J'ai _____-et-un ans: *I am 21*

b. Mon père a _____ -sept ans:
My father is fifty-seven

c. Ma mère a _____ -huit ans:
My mother is forty-eight

d. Mon grand-père a _____ ans:
My grandfather is one-hundred years old

e. Mon oncle a _____-deux ans:
My uncle is sixty-two

f. Ils ont _____ ans: *They are ninety*

g. Mes cousins ont _____-quatre ans:
My cousins are forty-four

h. Elle a _____ ans? *Is she seventy?*

4. Correct the translation errors

a. *My father is forty:* Mon père a quatorze ans

b. *My mother is fifty-two:* Ma mère a cinquante ans

c. *We are forty-two:* Nous avons quarante-douze ans

d. *I am forty-one:* J'ai quarante-un ans

e. *They are thirty-four:* Ils ont trente-deux ans

5. Translate into French (please write out the numbers in full French)

a. In my family, there are 4 people:

b. My mother is called Susanne and she is 43:

c. My father is called Pierre and he is 48:

d. My older sister is called Julie and she is 31:

e. My younger sister is called Amandine and she is18:

f. I am called Alice and I am 27:

g. My grandfather is called Anthony and he is 87:

Unit 5. Talking about my family + Counting to 100: Writing

1. Spot and correct the spelling mistakes

a. carante: *quarante*

b. trente-un:

c. quatre-vin-deux:

d. vingt et un:

e. quatre vingt dix:

f. sent:

g. soixante dix:

h. dix-six:

3. Rearrange the sentence below in the correct word order

a. ma Dans quatre famille personnes il y a
In my family there are four people

b. bien avec m'entends mon frère Je
I get along with my brother

c. père, Mon s'appelle deux qui Michel cinquante a - ans *My father, who is called Michel, is fifty-two*

d. père et moi Dans famille ma mon mère, il y a personnes: trois *In my family there are three people: my mother, my father and I*

e. s' Mon qui cousin, ans Yoan sept appelle - trente a *My cousin, who is called Yoan, is thirty-seven*

f. grand-père, vingt ans Fernand qui Mon - sept quatre a, s'appelle *My grandfather, who is called Fernand, is eighty-seven*

2. Complete with the missing letters

a. Ma m__re a quar__nte an_.

b. Mon pè__e a cin___ante-et-un a__s.

c. Mes gran___-parents ont quatre-_____ __ns.

d. M___ pet___ fr__re a vi__gt an__.

e. __a gra___-m__re a qua___-vin__-dix a__.

f. Mon gr___d f___e a trent__ ___s.

4. Complete

a. In my family: D____ m__ f_____

b. There are: I__ __ __

c. Who is called: Q___ s'a_____

d. My mother: M__ m_____

e. My father: M___ p_____

f. He is fifty: Il a c_____ a____

g. I am sixty: J'ai s_____ a____

h. He is forty: Il a q_____ a____

5. Write a sentence for each person as shown in the example for Paul

Mon meilleur ami s'appelle Paul et il a quinze ans. Je m'entends très bien avec lui.

Name	Relationship to me	Age	How I get along with them
Paul	best friend	15	very well
Benoît	father	57	not well
Martine	mother	45	very badly
Antoinette	aunt	60	well
André	uncle	67	not well
Michel	grandfather	75	very well

Revision Quickie 1:
Numbers 1-100, dates and birthdays, hair and eyes, family

1. Match up

11	quinze
12	douze
13	seize
14	dix-huit
15	onze
16	dix-neuf
17	quatorze
18	vingt
19	dix-sept
20	treize

2. Translate the dates into English

a. Le trente juin

b. Le premier juillet

c. Le quinze septembre

d. Le vingt-deux mars

e. Le trente-et-un décembre

f. Le cinq janvier

g. Le seize avril

h. Le vingt-neuf février

3. Complete with the missing words

a. Mon anniversaire _____ le quinze avril

b. J'ai quatorze _____

c. Mon frère ___ les cheveux _____

d. D'_____ es-tu?

e. Dans ma famille _____ quatre personnes

f. ____ mère a les _____ marron

g. Je suis ____ Québec

h. Mon frère s' _____ Robert

où	est	du	a	appelle
blonds	yeux	ans	il y a	ma

4. Write out the solution in words as shown in the example

a. quarante – trente = dix

b. trente – dix =

c. quarante + trente =

d. vingt x deux =

e. quatre-vingts moins vingt =

f. quatre-vingt-dix – cinquante =

g. trente x trois =

h. vingt + cinquante =

i. vingt plus trente =

5. Complete the words

a. Mon gr_____-_____ *My grandfather*

b. Ma c_____ *My female cousin*

c. Les y_____ v_____ *Green eyes*

d. La ba_____ *Beard*

e. Les lu_____ *Glasses*

f. Ma s_____ *My sister*

g. J'____ *I have*

6. Translate into English

a. Ma mère a les cheveux châtains.

b. J'ai les yeux bleus.

c. J'ai quarante ans.

d. Mon grand-père a quatre-vingt-dix ans.

e. Mon père porte des lunettes.

f. Mon frère a une moustache.

g. Mon frère a les cheveux noirs.

h. Ma sœur a les yeux gris.

UNIT 6: (Part 1/2)
Describing myself and another family member (physical and personality)

In this unit you will learn:
- What your immediate family members are like
- Useful adjectives to describe them
- The third person of the verb 'Être'(to be):
  'il est' (he is), 'elle est' (she is)
- All the persons of the verb 'Avoir' in the present indicative

You will also revisit
- Numbers from 1 to 31
- Hair and eyes description

UNIT 6 (Part 1/2)
Intro to describing myself and another family member

		MASCULINE	FEMININE
Je	**suis**	**beau** *handsome* **fort** *strong* **grand** *tall* **gros** *fat* **mince** *slim*	**belle** *pretty* **forte** *strong* **grande** *tall* **grosse** *fat* **mince** *slim*
Ma petite sœur *My little sister* **Mon grand frère** *My big brother* **Ma mère** *My mother* **Mon père** *My father*	**est**	**moche** *ugly* **musclé** *muscular* **petit** *short* **méchant** *mean* **ennuyeux** *boring* **généreux** *generous* **marrant** *fun* **sympathique** *nice* **têtu** *stubborn* **timide** *shy*	**moche** *ugly* **musclée** *muscular* **petite** *short* **méchante** *mean* **ennuyeuse** *boring* **généreuse** *generous* **marrante** *fun* **sympathique** *nice* **têtue** *stubborn* **timide** *shy*

Unit 6. Vocabulary building

1. Match

Je suis sympathique	I am fun
Je suis timide	I am slim
Je suis têtu	I am generous
Je suis beau	I am shy
Je suis marrant	I am nice
Je suis généreux	I am short
Je suis fort	I am strong
Je suis antipathique	I am good-looking
Je suis petit	I am unfriendly
Je suis grand	I am tall
Je suis mince	I am stubborn

2. Complete

a. Mon petit frère est m_____
My little brother is slim

b. Mon père est m_____ *My father is mean*

c. Ma grande sœur est t_____
My big sister is stubborn

d. Je suis m_____ *I am muscular*

e. Mon grand frère est m_____
My big brother is fun

f. Mon ami Paul est f_____
My friend Paul is strong

3. Categories – sort the adjectives below in the categories provided

a. fort; b. musclé; c. sympathique; d. têtu; e. belle;
f. intelligente; g. patiente; h. timide; i. généreux;
j. ennuyeux; k. gros; l. moche; m. marrant

Le physique	La personnalité

4. Complete the words

a. Je suis ennuy_ _ _ (m)

b. Je suis moc_ _ (m)

c. Je suis muscl_ _ (f)

d. Je suis tê_ _ (m)

e. Je suis peti_ _ (f)

f. Je suis fo_ _ (m)

g. Je suis sym_ _(f)

h. Je suis gr_ _ (m)

5. Translate into English

a. Ma grande sœur est généreuse.

b. Mon petit frère n'est pas gros.

c. Mon grand frère est ennuyeux.

d. Ma mère est marrante.

e. Je ne suis pas moche.

f. Je suis un peu têtu.

g. Je suis très beau.

h. Mon ami Valentin est fort.

6. Spot and correct the translation mistakes

a. Je suis fort: *He is strong*

b. Il est mince: *He is fat*

c. Je suis très belle: *I am very ugly*

d. Ma mère est grande: *My mother is short*

e. Mon chat est moche: *My cat is cute*

f. Ma sœur est têtue: *My sister is boring*

g. Mon père est méchant: *My father is nice*

7. Complete

a. M_ m_ _ _

b. M_ _ f_ _ _ _

c. M_ _ p_ _ _

d. M_ f_ _ _ _ _

e. Il e_t t_ _ _

f. M_ s_ _ _ _

8. English to French translation

a. I am strong and funny. (f)

b. My mother is very stubborn.

c. My sister is short and slim.

d. My brother is intelligent.

e. I am friendly and fun. (f)

f. My father is tall and a bit fat.

g. Gargamel is ugly and mean.

h. I am tall and muscular. (m)

Grammar Time 1: ÊTRE - To be (Part 1)

Masculine		
je	**suis** *I am*	bavard *talkative*
		fort
tu	**es** *you are*	grand
		gros
il		méchant
mon frère	**est** *he is*	mince
		patient
mon père		petit
		sympathique
nous		bavards *talkative*
mon père et moi	**sommes** *we are*	forts
		grands
vous	**êtes** *you guys are*	gros
		méchants
ils		minces
mes frères	**sont** *they are*	patients
		petits
mes parents		sympathiques
Feminine		
je	**suis** *I am*	bavarde *talkative*
		forte
tu	**es** *you are*	grande
		grosse
elle		méchante
ma sœur	**est** *she is*	mince
		patiente
ma mère		petite
		sympathique
nous		bavardes *talkative*
ma mère et moi (fem)	**sommes** *we are*	fortes
		grandes
vous	**êtes** *you girls are*	grosses
		méchantes
elles		minces
mes sœurs	**sont** *they are*	patientes
		petites
mes cousines		sympathiques

Present indicative of "Être" (to be) – Drills 1

1. Match up

Nous sommes	I am
Elles sont	You are
Je suis	He is
Tu es	They are
Vous êtes	We are
Il est	You guys are

2. Complete with the missing forms of 'Être'

a. Je _____ très bavard: *I am very talkative*

b. Ma mère _____ marrante: *My mother is funny*

c. Mes sœurs _____ bavardes: *My sisters are talkative*

d. Mon frère _____ très paresseux: *My brother is very lazy*

e. Mes parents _____ stricts: *My parents are strict*

f. Comment _____ tu? *What are you like?*

g. Comment _____ tes cheveux? *What is your hair like?*

h. _____ _____ très forts! *You guys are very strong!*

3. Translate into English

a. Mon père est sympathique.

b. Ma mère est bavarde.

c. Mes frères sont timides.

d. Ma petite sœur n'est pas très grande.

e. Mon meilleur ami est un peu gros.

f. Mon grand-père est très aimable.

g. Ma grande sœur est très grande.

h. Vous êtes très forts!

4. Complete with the missing letters

a. Nous som_ _ _ très sympathiques:

We are very nice

b. Ma mère e_ _ très stricte: *My mother is very strict*

c. Mes parents s_ _ _ très patients:

My parents are very patient

d. Mes cousins s_ _ _ très méchants:

My cousins are very mean

e. Ma sœur e_ _ très grosse: *My sister is very fat*

f. Vous ê_ _ _ très bavards!

You guys are very talkative!

g. Je _ _ _ _ un peu timide: *I am a bit shy*

h. Mes grands-parents s_ _ _ très aimables:

My grandparents are very likeable

i. Comment e_ -tu? *What are you like?*

5. Translate into French

a. You are: (tu) ___ ___

b. He is: (il) ___ ___ ___

c. You guys are: (vous) ___ ___ ___ ___

d. They (f) are: (elles) ___ ___ ___ ___

e. We are: (nous) ___ ___ ___ ___ ___ ___

f. She is: (elle) ___ ___ ___

6. Spot and correct the errors

a. Ma mère es très sympathique.

b. Mes parents sommes très patients et aimables.

c. Ma sœur es mince.

d. Ma sœur et moi sont grands.

e. Comment est-tu?

Present indicative of "Être" (to be) – Drills 2

7. Complete with the missing letters

a. Nous so_____es grands: *We are tall*

b. Tu e___ petit: *You are short*

c. Mon chat e____ gros: *My cat is fat*

d. Mes professeurs so_____ très patients: *My teachers are very patient*

e. ____ es très belle: *You are very pretty*

f. Je ne s____s pas timide: *I am not shy*

g. Mon frère et moi s___mmes très travailleurs: *My brother and I are very hard-working*

8. Complete with the missing forms of the verb Être

a. Ma mère _____

b. Mes parents _____

c. Je _____

d. Elles _____

e. Ma mère et moi _____

f. Mon frère _____

g. Toi et tes sœurs _____

h. Tu ____

i. Vous _____

9. Complete with the missing forms of ÊTRE

a. Je _____ de Martinique.

b. Ma mère _____ très grande et belle.

c. Mes parents _____ très stricts.

d. Mon frère _____ très ennuyeux.

e. Je _____ un peu gros.

f. Elles_____ petites.

g. Mon frère et moi _____ musclés.

h. Mon cousin Marco _____ italien.

i. Comment _____ ta sœur?

10. Translate into French. Make sure the <u>underlined words</u> have a feminine ending in French ('e')

a. My mother is <u>tall</u>

b. My father is short

c. My brother is ugly

d. My sister is <u>talkative</u>

e. My grandfather is strict

f. My grandmother is <u>patient</u>

g. My mother is <u>intelligent</u>

11. English to French translation. Remember that plural adjectives add an 'S' (e.g. *fort – forts*). Make sure that the <u>words underlined</u> end in 's' or 'es', as shown in the example:

a. My mother and my sister are very <u>**tall**</u>: Ma mère et ma sœur sont très grand<u>es</u>

b. My sisters are <u>**kind**</u> and <u>**patient**</u>:

c. My parents are very <u>**friendly**</u>:

d. I (F) am talkative and lazy:

e. My brother and I are very <u>**tall**</u>:

f. My mother and my sister are <u>**beautiful**</u>:

g. My girlfriend and her (sa) sister are very <u>**short**</u>:

Grammar Time 2: AVOIR – To have (Part 1)
(Present indicative)

j'	**ai** *I have*	**les cheveux** *the hair*	**blonds** *blonde* **châtains** *light brown* **noirs** *black* **roux** *red* **frisés** *curly* **mi-longs** *mid length* **ondulés** *wavy* **raides** *straight* **courts** *short* **longs** *long*
tu	**as** *you have*		
il **elle** **ma sœur** **mon frère** **ma mère** **mon père**	**a** *he/she has*		
nous **toi et moi** **ma mère et moi** **mon père et moi**	**avons** *we have*	**les yeux** *the eyes*	**bleus** *blue* **marron*** *brown* **noirs** *black* **verts** *green*
vous**	**avez** *you guys have*		
ils, elles **mes sœurs** **mes frères** **mes parents**	**ont** *they have*		

*Author's note: marron is invariable so it never changes, regardless of gender or number
** vous avez can refer to a group of guys or ladies. It is also the polite form for "you".

Verb drills

1. Translate into English

a. Nous avons les cheveux noirs.

b. Il a les cheveux blonds.

c. Elles ont les cheveux très longs.

d. Tu as les cheveux très courts.

e. Ils ont les yeux verts.

f. Il a les cheveux roux.

g. Nous avons les cheveux frisés.

h. Il a les cheveux mi-longs et raides.

2. Spot and correct the mistakes (note: not all sentences are wrong)

a. Ma mère a les cheveux blonds.

b. Mes frères avez les cheveux gris.

c. J'a les cheveux longs.

d. Il ont les cheveux courts.

e. Nous avons les cheveux court.

f. Mes parents ont les cheveux frisés.

3. Complete with the missing verb

a. J'___ les cheveux blonds.

b. Ma mère ___ les yeux bleus.

c. Mes sœurs ___ les cheveux roux.

d. Ma mère ___ les cheveux gris.

e. Nous _____ les cheveux noirs.

f. Mon grand-père ___ les cheveux blancs.

g. Ma mère et moi _____ les cheveux blancs.

h. Mon cousin ___ les cheveux châtains.

i. Vous ____ les cheveux longs?

j. Mon frère et moi _____ les cheveux frisés.

k. Mon ami Paul ___ les yeux verts.

l. Mes frères ____ les cheveux courts.

m. J'___ les cheveux mi-longs.

n. Tu ___ les cheveux longs comme ta mère?

4. Complete with: *a, avons* or *ont*

a. Ma mère _____ les cheveux blonds.

b. Mes parents _____ les yeux marron.

c. Ma grande sœur et moi _____ les cheveux noirs.

d. Mes grands-parents _____ les cheveux noirs.

e. Mes parents _____ les cheveux blonds.

f. Mes sœurs _____ les cheveux frisés.

g. Ma petite sœur et moi ____ les cheveux ondulés.

h. Mon cousin _____ les cheveux roux.

i. Mes deux sœurs _____ les cheveux raides.

j. Mon amie Nicole et moi _____ les yeux bleus.

5. Translate into French

a. We have black hair.

b. You have long hair.

c. You guys have blue eyes.

d. She has green eyes.

e. My father has curly hair.

f. My sister has straight hair.

g. My uncle has grey hair.

h. My grandfather has no hair.

i. My father and I have blonde hair.

j. My uncle Paul has green eyes.

6. Guided writing: write a text in the first person singular (I) including the details below:

- Say you are 9 years old.
- Say you have a brother and a sister.
- Say your brother is 15.
- Say he has brown, straight, short hair and green eyes.
- Say he is tall and handsome.
- Say you have a sister.
- Say she is 12.
- Say she has black, curly, long hair and brown eyes.
- Say your parents are short, have light brown hair and brown eyes.

7. Write an 80 to 100 words text in which you describe four people you know very well relative of friends. You must include their:

a. Name

b. Age

c. Hair (colour, length and type)

d. Eye colour

e. If they wear glasses or not

f. Their physical description

g. Their personality description

UNIT 6 (Part 2/2)
Describing my family and saying why I like/dislike them

Dans ma famille j'ai *In my family I have…*			
Dans ma famille il y a <u>quatre</u> personnes *There are <u>four</u> persons in my family…*	**mon grand-père, Claude** *my grandfather Claude*	**J'aime "mon _____"** **car il est…** *I like my _____ because he is…*	**amusant** *fun* **beau** *handsome* **fort** *strong* **généreux** *generous* **grand** *tall*
	mon père, Georges *my father Georges*		**gros** *fat*
	mon oncle, Paul *my uncle Paul*	**"Mon père est très/assez…** *My dad is very/quite…*	**honnête** *honest* **intelligent** *clever* **méchant** *mean*
Je m'entends bien avec… *I get along well with…*	**mon petit/grand frère, Olivier** *my little/big brother Olivier*		**mince** *slim* **petit** *short* **sympa** *nice*
	mon cousin, Tristan *my -boy- cousin Tristan*	**"Mon père" est aussi un peu…** *My dad is also a bit…*	**timide** *shy* **têtu** *stubborn*
Je m'entends mal avec… *I get along badly with…*			
	ma grand-mère, Thérèse *my grandmother Thérèse*	**J'aime "ma _____"** **car elle est…** *I like my _____ because she is…*	**amusante** *fun* **belle** *pretty* **forte** *strong* **généreuse** *generous* **grande** *tall*
	ma mère, Éliane *my mother Éliane*		**grosse** *fat*
	ma tante, Françoise *my aunt Françoise*	**"Ma mère" est très/assez…** *My mum is very/quite …*	**honnête** *honest* **intelligente** *clever* **méchante** *mean*
	ma petite/grande sœur, Léa *my little/big sister Léa*		**mince** *slim* **petite** *short* **sympa** *nice*
	ma cousine, Claire *my -girl- cousin Claire*	**"Ma mère" est aussi un peu…** *My mum is also a bit …*	**timide** *shy* **têtue** *stubborn*

Unit 6. Describing my family: VOCABULARY BUILDING

1. Complete with the missing word

a. Dans ma famille j'_____: *In my family I have...*

b. J'ai _____ personnes: *I have four people...*

c. Ma _____, Angèle: *My mother, Angèle*

d. Je m'entends _____ avec ma…
I get along well with my...

e. Je m'entends _____ avec mon…
I get along badly with my...

f. Mon oncle_____ très grand et…
My uncle is very tall and...

2. Match up

Ma tante	My cousin f
Mon grand-père	My grandad
Ma mère	My mum
Mon père	My dad
Mon grand frère	My aunt
Mon cousin	My little bro
Mon petit frère	My big bro
Mon oncle	My uncle
Ma sœur	My sister
Ma cousine	My cousin m

3. Translate into English

a. J'aime mon oncle:

b. Ma cousine est généreuse:

c. Elle a les cheveux blonds:

d. Je m'entends bien avec elle:

e. Je n'aime pas mon frère:

f. Je m'entends mal avec…

g. Il est têtu:

h. Tu es tranquille:

4. Add the missing letter

a. t__tu   c. __ympathique   e. __ousin   g. g__and   i. auss__   k. j'a__me

b. je m'__ntends   d. __rand-père   f. __etit   h. m__re   j. __ncle   l. parc__ que

5. Broken words

a. D____ m__ fam____ j'___ : *In my family I have*

b. Q_____ p_____ : *Four people*

c. M__ m_____ e__ t_____ s_____ :
My mother is very nice

d. J__ m'_____ b_____ a____ m__ m_____ :
I get on well with my mother

e. M__ o_____ e__ t____ g_____ :
My uncle is very generous

f. J__ m'_____ m__ a_____ m__ p_____ :
I get on badly with my father

g. M__ s_____ a l__ c_____ l_____ :
My sister has long hair

h. E____ e___ t_____ : *She is stubborn*

6. Complete with a suitable word

a. J'ai quatre _____.

b. _____ sympathique.

c. Je _____ bien.

d. Elle est très _____.

e. Il a les _____ blonds.

f. ____ aime ma mère.

g. Je m'entends _____ avec mon oncle.

h. Elle a les cheveux noirs et_____.

i. Il a les _____bleus.

j. Mon cousin est_____ marrant.

k. Ma _____ est très intelligente.

Unit 6. Describing my family: READING

Je suis Charles. J'ai dix ans et je vis à Kuala Lumpur, la capitale de la Malaisie. Dans ma famille j'ai cinq personnes, mon père Jean, ma mère Anne et mes deux frères, David et Pierre. Je m'entends bien avec David car il est sympa et généreux. Par contre, je m'entends mal avec Pierre car il est très têtu.

Je m'appelle Véronique. J'ai quatorze ans et je vis à Marseille, dans le sud de la France. J'aime beaucoup mon grand-père car il est très marrant. Il est intelligent, mais très timide.
Mon père, est assez gros et très têtu. Il a les yeux marron et les cheveux rasés.

Je m'appelle Emmanuel. J'ai quinze ans et je vis en Normandie, dans le nord-ouest de la France. J'ai les cheveux blonds et rasés. Dans ma famille, il y a six personnes. Je ne m'entends pas bien avec ma sœur car elle est stupide et têtue. Je m'entends très bien avec mes cousins car ils sont très sympathiques.
Mon cousin préféré s'appelle Yann et il est grand et fort. Il est très amusant et sympa. Il a les cheveux noirs et courts et porte des lunettes.

Je suis Pierre Pujos. J'ai dix ans et je vis à Paris, la capitale de la France. Je suis très beau. Dans ma famille, il y a beaucoup de personnes, huit au total. J'aime mon oncle, mais je n'aime pas ma tante. Je m'entends très bien avec mon oncle Éric car il est marrant et sympa. Par contre, ma tante est antipathique et méchante.
Ma tante Marie a les cheveux blonds, longs et frisés et les yeux bleus comme moi. Son anniversaire est le cinq mai.

Je m'appelle Georges. J'ai neuf ans et je vis à Toulouse, en France. Dans ma famille, j'ai quatre personnes. Je m'entends mal avec mon père car il est très têtu et antipathique. J'aime beaucoup ma grand-mère car elle est très généreuse et elle est aussi amusante.

1. Find the French for the following in Véronique's text

a. I am called:

b. In the south:

c. My grandfather:

d. But:

e. Very:

f. My father:

g. Brown eyes:

h. Shaved hair:

2. Answer the following questions about Pierre's text

a. How old is he?

b. Where is he from?

c. How many people are there in his family?

d. Who does he get along well with?

e. Why does he like Éric?

f. Who does he not like?

g. When is her birthday?

h. What's his family name?

3. Complete with the missing words

Je m'appelle Alexandra. _____ dix ans et je vis _____ Biarritz. Dans ma famille, j'ai quatre _____. Je _____ bien avec mon grand-père car il ____ très sympa et amusant. Mon père a les _____ courts et les _____ verts.

4. Find someone who? – answer the questions below about all 5 texts

a. Who has a grandma who is very generous?

b. Who is fifteen years old?

c. Who celebrates their birthday on 5 May?

d. Who has a favourite cousin?

e. Who is from the south of France?

f. Who only gets along well with one of his brothers?

g. Who has a shaved head very short hair?

h. Who is a bit mean?

Unit 6. Describing my family: TRANSLATION

1. Faulty translation: spot and correct any translation mistakes (in the English)

a. Dans ma famille il y a quatre personnes:
In my family there are fourteen people

b. Ma mère, Anne et mon frère David:
My mother Anne and my cousin David

c. Je m'entends mal avec mon père:
I get on well with my father

d. Mon oncle s'appelle Yvon:
My father is called Yvon

e. Yvon est très sympa et amusant:
Yvon is very mean and fun

f. Yvon a les cheveux rasés: *Ivan has long hair*

2. Translate from French to English

a. J'aime mon grand-père.

b. Ma grand-mère est très sympathique.

c. Mon cousin a les cheveux rasés.

d. Je m'entends bien avec mon grand frère.

e. Je m'entends très mal avec ma cousine.

f. J'adore ma grand-mère car elle est généreuse.

g. Mon père est sympa et amusant.

h. Je n'aime pas ma petite sœur.

i. Je m'entends mal avec mon cousin Éric parce qu'il est stupide.

3. Phrase-level translation

a. He is nice:

b. She is generous:

c. I get along well with:

d. I get along badly with:

e. My uncle is fun:

f. My little brother:

g. I like my cousin Marie:

h. She has short and black hair:

i. He has blue eyes:

j. I don't like my grandfather:

k. He is very stubborn:

4. Sentence-level translation

a. My name is Pierre Pujos. I am nine years old. In my family, I have four people.

b. My name is Carla. I have blue eyes. I get along well with my brother.

c. I get along badly with my brother because he is stubborn.

d. My name is Frank. I live in France. I do not like my uncle David because he is mean.

e. I like my cousin a lot because she is very nice.

f. In my family, I have five people. I like my father, but I do not like my mother.

Unit 6. Describing my family: WRITING

1. Split sentences

Mon père est	les cheveux noirs
Ma mère est	bien avec elle
Elle a les	mon oncle
Il a	sympathique
Je n'aime pas	yeux verts
J'aime beaucoup ma	tante
Je m'entends	généreuse

2. Rewrite the sentences in the correct order

a. dans ma six j'ai famille personnes

b. je avec mon m'entends bien frère

c. n' mon je aime oncle pas

d. ma les yeux mère a bleus

e. ma et sympa tante est amusante

3. Spot and correct the grammar and spelling errors

a. Dans ma famille j'as

b. Je m'entend bien avec

c. Je n'aime pas mon tante

d. Mon frère est amusante

e. Je m'entends mall avec

f. Mon père est généreuse

g. Elle a les yeu bleu

h. Ma sœur est très têtu

i. Il a le cheveu rasés

j. Je aime beaucoup mon oncle

4. Anagrams

a. fimalle =

b. cimne =

c. esgros =

d. lbele =

e. inlligtente =

f. myspa =

g. tutê =

h. santeamu =

5. Guided writing: write 3 short paragraphs describing the people below in the first person

Name	Age	Family	Likes	Likes	Dislikes
Paul	12	4 people	mother – very nice – long blond hair	older brother – because fun and very kind	cousin Emma – because very mean and selfish
Léon	11	5 people	father –very fun – short black hair	grandmother – because very nice and generous	uncle Édouard– because stubborn and ugly
Michel	10	3 people	grandfather – very funny – very short hair	younger sister – because very nice and shy	aunt Caroline – very strong but stubborn

6. Describe this person in the third person

Name: uncle Anthony

Hair: blond, shaved

Eyes: blue

Opinion: like him a lot

Physical: tall and strong

Personality: nice, fun, generous

THE LANGUAGE GYM

UNIT 7
Talking about pets

Grammar Time: AVOIR (pets and description)
Questions skills: age/descriptions/pets

In this unit you will learn how to say in French
- what pets you have at home
- what pet you would like to have
- what their name is
- some more adjectives to describe appearance and personality
- key question words

You will also learn how to ask questions about
- Name / age / appearance / quantity

You will revisit the following
- Introducing oneself
- Family members
- Describing people
- The verb 'Avoir' (to have) in the present indicative

UNIT 7
Talking about pets

À la maison, j'ai / Chez moi, j'ai / *At home I have* Je n'ai pas <u>de</u> / *I don't have* Mon ami Denis a… / *My friend Denis has…*	un canard *a duck* un chat *a cat* un cheval *a horse* un chien *a dog* un cochon d'Inde *a guinea pig* un hamster *a hamster* un lapin *a rabbit* un oiseau *a bird* un perroquet *a parrot* un poisson *a fish* un serpent *a snake*	qui s'appelle **Bronco** / *that is called Bronco* **il est** / *he/it is*	**petit** *small* **grand** *big* **jaune** *yellow* **bleu** *blue* **blanc** *white* **orange** *orange* **noir** *black* **rouge** *red* **vert** *green* **barbant** *boring* **joli** *pretty* **amusant** *fun* **moche** *ugly* **rigolo** *funny* **intelligent** *clever*
Je voudrais avoir / *I would like to have* Je ne voudrais pas avoir <u>de</u> / *I wouldn't like to have*	**une araignée** *a spider* **une perruche** *a budgie* **une souris** *a mouse* **une tortue** *a turtle/tortoise*	qui s'appelle **Lola** / *that is called Lola* **elle est** / *she/it is*	**petite** *small* **grande** *big* **jaune** *yellow* **bleue** *blue* **blanche** *white* **orange** *orange* **noire** *black* **rouge** *red* **verte** *green* **barbante** *boring* **jolie** *pretty* **amusante** *fun* **moche** *ugly* **rigolote** *funny* **intelligente** *clever*

Author's note: in the negative form in French the "un" or "une" turns into "de"
Examples: - Je <u>n'</u>ai <u>pas</u> <u>de</u> lapin (*I don't have a rabbit*)

THE LANGUAGE GYM

Unit 7. Talking about pets: VOCABULARY BUILDING

1. Complete with the missing words

a. Chez moi, j'ai un o_____ :
At home I have a bird

b. Je n'ai pas de l_____ : *I don't have a rabbit*

c. Je voudrais avoir un c_____ : *I'd like to have a dog*

d. Je ne voudrais pas avoir de t_____ :
I wouldn't like to have a turtle

e. C_____ moi, j'ai un c_____ : *At home I have a cat*

f. Je n'ai pas de s_____ : *I don't have a snake*

g. J'____ une araignée chez moi: *I have a spider at home*

h. Je v_____ avoir un cheval: *I'd like to have a horse*

2. Match up

un chat	a duck
un chien	a mouse
un cheval	two fish
un oiseau	a cat
un poisson	a turtle
une tortue	a fish
une souris	a guinea pig
un perroquet	a dog
deux poissons	a parrot
un canard	a bird
un cochon d'Inde	a horse

3. Translate into English

a. J'ai un chien.

b. Mon amie Léa a un canard.

c. J'ai deux poissons.

d. Je n'ai pas d'animal chez moi.

e. J'ai trois chiens.

f. Je voudrais avoir un cochon d'Inde.

g. Mon frère a une tortue.

h. Mon chat a cinq ans.

4. Add the missing letter

a. Mon am__e

b. Une tort__e

c. Un __erroquet

d. Deux poisson__

e. Un p__isson

f. Un __apin

g. Un can__rd

h. Un c__eval

5. Anagrams

a. neihC = Chien

b. hatC =

c. uetTor =

d. ioPsson =

e. risSou =

f. nardCa =

g. gnéerAai =

h. valChe =

6. Broken words

a. C_____ m____ j'__ u__ c_____ :
At home I have a dog

b. M___ a_____Paul a u__ p_____ :
My friend Paul has a parrot

c. M___ f_____ a u____ t_____ :
My brother has a turtle

d. J___ n'___ p___ de l_____ :
I don't have a rabbit

e. J'___u_____ s_____ :
I have a snake

7. Complete with a suitable word

a. J'ai dix _____.

b. Mon poisson s'_____ Nemo.

c. Mon _____ Paul a un chien.

d. Mon frère ___une souris.

e. Chez_____ j'ai deux animaux.

f. _____moi, j'ai deux animaux: un chien et une _____.

g. Chez moi j'ai _____ lapins.

h. Chez moi j'ai ____ souris.

i. J'ai _____ canards.

THE LANGUAGE GYM

Unit 7. Talking about pets: READING

Je m'appelle Hélène. J'ai huit ans et je vis à Paris. Dans ma famille, il y a quatre personnes: mes parents, mon petit frère qui s'appelle Michel et moi. Michel est très méchant et ennuyeux. Nous avons deux animaux: un chien qui s'appelle Biscotte et un chat qui s'appelle Caramel. Biscotte est très mignon. Caramel est très méchant. Comme mon frère!

Je m'appelle Robert. J'ai neuf ans et je vis à Mende. Dans ma famille, il y a quatre personnes: mes parents, mon grand frère qui s'appelle Francis, et moi. Francis a douze ans et il est très joueur. Nous avons deux animaux: un perroquet qui s'appelle Coco et un chat qui s'appelle Frimousse. Coco est très bavard. Frimousse est très joueur, comme mon frère.

Je m'appelle Jules. J'ai neuf ans et je vis à La Rochelle. Dans ma famille il y a cinq personnes: mes parents et mes deux frères, qui s'appelle Léo et Tanguy. Léo est très bavard et marrant. Tanguy est très sérieux et travailleur. Nous avons deux animaux à la maison: un lapin qui s' appelle Ben et une tortue qui s' appelle Sam. Le lapin est très amusant et énergique. Sam est très sérieuse, comme mon frère Tanguy.

Je m'_____ Paul. J'ai onze a___ et je v_____ à Biarritz. C____ moi, il y a cinq personnes: mes parents, m____ deux s_____ qui s' appellent Anna et Martine, et moi. Anna e___ très bavarde et aimable. Martine est t____ paresseuse et mé_____. Nous a_____ deux animaux chez nous: une souris q___ s'appelle Maya et un chat qui s'_____ Swift. Swift est t____ marrant et énergique. Maya e___ très aimable, c_____ ma s_____ Anna.

Je m'appelle Solène. J'ai dix ans. Dans ma famille il y a quatre personnes: mes parents et mes deux petites sœurs, qui s'appellent Sandrine et Louise. Sandrine est très généreuse et serviable. Louise est très têtue et ennuyeuse. Nous avons deux animaux: un lapin qui s'appelle Bunny et un canard qui s'appelle Ducko. Bunny est très tranquille et aimable. Ducko est très bruyant et énergique.

1. Find the French for the following in Hélène's text

a. two pets

b. which is called

c. a cat

d. a dog

e. very cute

f. like my brother

g. my parents

h. my name is

i. very mean

j. four people

2. Find someone who? Answer the questions below about Hélène, Robert, Solène and Jules

a. has a cat?

b. has parrot?

c. has a duck?

d. has a turtle?

e. has a rabbit?

f. has a dog?

3. Answer the following questions about Jules' text

a. Where does Jules live?

b. What is his brother Tanguy like?

c. Who is fun and lively?

d. Who is like Tanguy?

e. Who is Sam?

f. Who is Ben?

g. Who is Léo?

4. Fill in the table below

Name	Hélène	Robert
Age		
City		
Pets		
Description of pets		

Unit 7. Talking about pets: TRANSLATION

1. Faulty translation: spot and correct any translation mistakes you find below

a. Dans ma famille il y a quatre personnes et deux animaux.
In my family there are four people and three pets.

b. Chez nous, nous avons deux animaux: un chien et une souris.
At home we have two pets: a dog and a rabbit.

c. Mon ami Paul a une tortue qui s'appelle Kura. Kura est très amusante.
My friend Paul has a duck called Kura. Kura is very boring.

d. Mon frère a un cheval qui s'appelle Flash.
My sister has a parrot called Flash.

e. Ma mère a un cochon d'Inde qui s'appelle Nicole. *My father has a frog called Nicole.*

f. J'ai un chat qui s'appelle Terreur. Terreur est très énergique. *I have a dog called Terreur. Terreur is very beautiful.*

2. Translate into English

a. Un chat joueur:

b. Un chien mignon:

c. Un canard amusant:

d. Une tortue ennuyeuse:

e. Un beau cheval:

f. Une souris énergique:

g. Un cochon d'Inde curieux:

h. J'ai deux animaux:

i. Chez moi, nous avons des animaux:

j. J'aimerais avoir un chien:

k. J'aimerais avoir un poisson:

l. J'ai une tortue, mais je voudrais avoir un serpent:

3. Phrase-level translation En to Fr

a. A boring dog:

b. A brown duck:

c. At home:

d. We have:

e. A beautiful horse:

f. A curious cat:

g. I have:

h. I don't have:

i. I would like to have:

4. Sentence-level translation En to Fr

a. My brother has a horse who is called Raya.

b. My sister has an ugly turtle who is called Nicole.

c. I have a fat hamster called Grassouillet.

d. At home we have three pets: a duck, a rabbit and a parrot.

e. I have a mouse called Sam.

f. At home we have three pets: a cat, a dog and a hamster.

g. I have two fish which are called Nemo and Dory.

Unit 7. Talking about pets: WRITING

1. Split sentences

J'ai un chien qui	chat blanc
Chez nous, nous avons	avoir une araignée
J'ai une souris	s'appelle Bandit
J'ai un	tortue
J'aimerais	deux animaux
Ma sœur a une	chez moi
Je n'ai pas d'animaux	noire

2. Rewrite the sentences in the correct order

a. animaux avons nous À maison trois la

b. une aimerais avoir J' souris

c. un J'ai chat un chien et

d. oiseau ami noir Mon a Paul un

e. Coco vert un qui avons Nous s' perroquet appelle

f. deux Nous bleus poissons avons

g. a sœur une qui s'appelle Ma Kura tortue

3. Spot and correct the grammar and spelling note: in several cases a word is missing

a. Chez moi un chat un chien

b. J'ai une souris noir

c. J'aimerais avoir serpent

d. Ma sœur ai un chat blanc

e. Mon ami Pierre a deux poisson

f. Mon cheval appelle Raya

g. J'ai une cheval marron

h. Chez moi, nous avons deux canard

4. Anagrams

a. iench =

b. tach =

c. sirous =

d. darcan =

e. pinla =

f. tuetor =

g. seauoi =

6. Describe this person in the third person:

Name: Robert

Hair: blonde, short

Eyes: green

Personality: very nice

Physical: short, fat

Pets: a dog, a cat and two fish and would like to have a spider

5. Guided writing – write 3 short paragraphs (in 1st person) describing the pets below using the details in the box

Name	Animal	Age	Colour	Character or appearance
Paul	dog	4	white	affectionate
Léon	duck	6	blue	funny
Michel	horse	1	brown	beautiful

 THE LANGUAGE GYM

Grammar Time 3: AVOIR (Part 2)
(Pets and description)

1. Translate

a. I have: J'___ ___

b. You have: t__ a __

c. He has: ___ ___ a

d. She has: elle ___

e. We have: n___ ___s ___ ___ ___ ___ ___

f. You guys have: vo___ ___ a___ ___ ___

g. They (M): ils ___ ___ ___

h. They (F): ___ ___ ___ ___ ___ ont

2. Translate into English

a. J'ai un très beau cheval.

b. Mon frère a un chat très moche.

c. Ma mère a un chien très amusant.

d. Mes cousins ont un très gros hamster.

e. Chez moi, nous avons un canard très bruyant.

f. Mon ami Paul a une très grande tortue.

g. Ma sœur Marie a un oiseau jaune.

3. Complete

a. I have a guinea pig: *J'____ un cochon d'Inde*

b. It is two years old: *Il ___ deux ans*

c. We have a turtle. It is 4 years old: *Nous _____ une tortue. Elle ___ quatre ans*

d. My sister has a dog: *Ma sœur ____ un chien*

e. My uncles have two cats: *Mes oncles _____ deux chats*

f. They are three years old: *Ils _____ trois ans*

g. My brother and I have a snake: *Mon frère et moi _____ un serpent*

h. Do you guys have pets? *Vous _____ des animaux?*

i. What animals do you have? *Quels animaux avez-_____?*

4. Translate into French

a. I have a guinea pig. It is three years old.

b. We don't have pets at home.

c. My dog is three years old. It is very big.

d. I have three brothers. They are very mean.

e. My cousins have a duck and a guinea pig.

f. My aunt has blond, curly and long hair. She is very pretty.

g. My brother and I have black hair and green eyes.

Question Skills 1: Age/descriptions/pets

1. Match question and answer

Quel âge as-tu?	Ils ont quatre-vingts ans.
Pourquoi tu ne t'entends pas bien avec ta mère?	Ça va bien, merci.
Comment sont ses cheveux?	J'ai quinze ans.
Quel âge ont tes grands-parents?	C'est le vert.
De quelle couleur sont tes yeux?	Car elle est très stricte.
Quelle est ta couleur préférée?	C'est le chien.
Comment vas-tu?	Je suis sympa et bavard.
Tu as des animaux?	Non, parce qu'il est méchant et paresseux.
Quel est ton animal préféré?	C'est le vingt juin.
Combien d'animaux as-tu?	Elle a les cheveux roux.
Comment est ta personnalité?	Ils sont bleus.
Comment es-tu physiquement?	J'en ai deux. Un chat et un perroquet.
Tu t'entends bien avec ton père?	Non, je n'en ai pas.
Quelle est la date de ton anniversaire?	Je suis petit et un peu gros.

2. Complete with the missing words

a. D'___ es-tu?
Where are you from?

b. _____ est Marie (de caractère)?
What is Marie like (personality-wise)?

c. _____ âge a ton père?
How old is your father?

d. Tu t' _____ bien avec ta mère?
Do you get along with your mum?

e. Quelle est la date de ton _____?
When is your birthday?

f. _____ est ton chien?
What is your dog like?

g. _____ d'animaux as-tu?
How many pets do you have?

3. Translate the following question words into English

a. Quel?

b. Quand?

c. Où?

d. Comment?

e. D'où?

f. Qui?

g. Combien?

h. Pourquoi?

i. Quelle?

5. Translate into French

a. What is your name?

b. How old are you?

c. What is your hair like?

d. What is your favourite animal?

e. Do you get along with your father?

f. Why don't you get along with your mother?

g. How many pets do you have?

h. Where are you from?

4. Complete

a. Q_____ â_____ as-tu?

b. D'___ es-___?

c. C_____ e___ t___ p_____?

d. Q_____ e___ t___ a_____ p_____?

e. C_____ d'_____ as-tu?

f. C_____ s___ t__ c_____?

g. T__ t'_____ b____ a___ t_ p___?

UNIT 8
Saying what jobs people do, why they like/dislike then and where they work

Grammar Time: -ER verbs travailler

In this unit you will learn how to say in French:
- What jobs people do
- Why they like/dislike those jobs
- Where they work
- Adjectives to describe jobs
- Words for useful jobs
- Words for types of buildings
- The full conjugation of the verb 'Travailler' (to work) in the present indicative

You will revisit the following:
- Family members
- The full conjugation of the verb 'Être' (to be)
- Description of people and pets

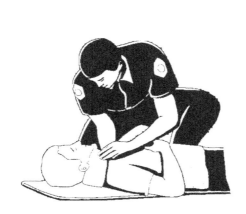

UNIT 8
Saying what jobs people do, why they like/dislike then and where they work

				Il/elle travaille dans… *he/she works in…*
Mon père *My father* **Mon frère** *My brother* **Mon oncle** *My uncle*	**est** *is* **travaille comme** *works as a*	**acteur** *actor* **avocat** *lawyer* **coiffeur** *hairdresser* **comptable** *accountant* **cuisinier** *chef* **fermier** *farmer* **homme au foyer** *househusband* **homme d'affaires** *businessman* **infirmier** *nurse* **ingénieur** *engineer* **mécanicien** *mechanic* **médecin** *doctor* **professeur** *teacher*	**il/elle aime cela car c'est** *he/she likes it because it is* **il/elle n'aime pas cela car c'est** *he/she doesn't like it because it is*	**actif** *active* **amusant** *funny* **barbant** *boring* **difficile** *difficult* **divertissant** *entertaining* **gratifiant** *rewarding*	**un atelier** *a workshop* **un bureau** *an office* **la campagne** *the countryside* **un collège** *a school* **une entreprise** *a company* **une ferme** *a farm* **un garage** *a garage*
Ma mère *My mother* **Ma grande sœur** *My big sister* **Ma tante** *My aunt*	**est** *is* **travaille comme** *works as a*	**actrice** *actress* **avocate** *lawyer* **coiffeuse** *hairdresser* **comptable** *accountant* **cuisinière** *chef* **femme au foyer** *housewife* **femme d'affaires** *businesswoman* **fermière** *farmer* **infirmière** *nurse* **ingénieure** *engineer* **mécanicienne** *mechanic* **médecin** *doctor* **professeure** *teacher*	**il/elle adore cela car c'est** *he/she loves it because it is* **il/elle déteste cela car c'est** *he/she hates it because it is*	**intéressant** *interesting* **stimulant** *stimulating* **stressant** *stressful* **très facile** *very easy*	**un hôtel** *a hotel* **la maison** *at home* **un restaurant** *a restaurant* **un théâtre** *a theatre* **la ville** *the city*

Unit 8. Saying what jobs people do: VOCABULARY BUILDING

1. Complete with the missing word

a. Mon père est_____ : *My father is a lawyer*

b. Ma mère est _____ : *My mother is a hairdresser*

c. Mon frère travaille comme _____ :
My brother works as a mechanic

d. Ma grand-mère est_____ : *My grandmother is a doctor*

e. Ma _____ sœur travaille comme _____ :
My big sister works as an engineer

f. Ma tante est _____ : *My aunt is an accountant*

g. Mon _____ est _____ *My uncle is a farmer*

2. Match up

c'est ennuyeux	it's stressful
c'est actif	entertaining
c'est difficile	it's difficult
divertissant	it's active
c'est stimulant	it's rewarding
c'est stressant	it's boring
c'est facile	it's interesting
c'est gratifiant	it's easy
c'est intéressant	it's stimulating

3. Translate into English

a. Ma mère est mécanicienne.

b. Il aime son travail.

c. Il travaille dans un garage.

d. Mon frère est comptable.

e. Elle n'aime pas son travail.

f. Mon cousin est coiffeur.

g. Elle adore son travail.

h. Car c'est amusant.

4. Add the missing letter

a. C'est f__cile

b. Ell__ aime

c. Ing__nieur

d. __édecin

e. C'est __tressant

f. T__availle comme

g. Elle est in__irmière

h. Mon o__cle

5. Anagrams

a. reimFer: *Fermier*

b. catAvo:

c. cinéMde:

d. ruetcA:

e. rAiecct:

f. Coblempta:

g. ffoiceur:

h. mièreinifr:

6. Broken words

a. M___ p_____ e___ h_____ a___ f_____ :
My dad is a househusband

b. I__ a_____ s____ t_____ :
He likes his job

c. M___ f_____ e___ f_____ :
My brother is a farmer

d. I__ t_____ à la c_____ :
He works in the countryside

e. E_____ d_____ s___ t_____ :
She hates her job

f. P_____ q__ c'____ a_____ :
Because it is active

7. Complete with a suitable word

a. Ma mère est _____.

b. Il _____ son travail.

c. Il aime cela car c'est _____.

d. Elle travaille dans un _____.

e. Ma _____ est coiffeuse.

f. Elle n' _____ pas son travail.

g. Parce que c'est très
_____.

h. _____ tante est médecin.

i. Elle aime son _____.

j. Mon oncle est mécanicien, il
travaille dans un _____.

Unit 8. Saying what jobs people do: READING

Je m'appelle Philippe. J'ai vingt ans et je vis à Casablanca au Maroc. Dans ma famille il y a quatre personnes. J'ai un chien très amusant, Snoopy. Ma mère travaille comme médecin en ville. Elle aime son travail car c'est gratifiant et actif. Mon oncle Daniel est fermier et il adore son travail. Parfois, c'est un travail dur et difficile, mais il adore les animaux.

Je m'appelle Sébastien. Dans ma famille il y a quatre personnes. Mon père s'appelle Matéo et il est avocat. Il aime son travail car c'est intéressant. Par contre, des fois c'est stressant. Ma mère est femme au foyer et elle aime assez son travail. Elle dit que c'est très gratifiant. Chez nous, nous avons un chien qui s'appelle Yoyo. Il est très grand et amusant! Je n'aime pas les chats.

Je m'appelle Sam. Je suis de Nice. Ma personne favorite dans ma famille, c'est ma mère. Elle est timide, mais très sympa. Ma mère est ingénieure mais maintenant elle ne travaille pas. Elle déteste mon oncle, il est intelligent, mais très méchant. Mon oncle est professeur mais il déteste son travail car c'est difficile et ennuyeux. Il travaille dans un collège, mais déteste les enfants. Chez lui, il a une tortue.

Je m'_____ Mariana. J'ai treize a__ et je v__ à Biscarosse. Dans ma f_____ il y a cinq personnes. Mon cousin Christophe e___ très bavard et aimable, il a trente ans. Christophe est pr_____ et il travaille dans un c_____. Il habite à Berlin en Allemagne. Il aime son t_____, car c'est int_____et gra_____. Chez moi, j'___ un animal qui s'_____Tara. C'est une ara_____: une mygale!

Je m'appelle Camille. Dans ma famille il y a quatre personnes. Ma mère s'appelle Valérie et elle est coiffeuse. Elle aime son travail car c'est intéressant et actif. Mon père est homme au foyer mais il n'aime pas beaucoup son travail car il dit que c'est très difficile et un peu ennuyeux. Nous n'avons pas d'animal, mais j'aimerais avoir un cheval. Mon cousin a un cheval qui s'appelle Furie et il est grand et fort. Quelle chance!

1. Find the French for the following in Philippe's text

a. I am 20

b. I have a dog

c. My dad works as…

d. A doctor

e. In the city

f. She likes her work

g. It is rewarding

h. Sometimes

i. He loves his work

j. Hard and difficult

2. Answer the questions on ALL texts

a. Who is Christophe?

b. Whose dad is a househusband?

c. Who has an uncle that is in the wrong job?

d. Whose mother is a doctor?

e. Who has a dog that doesn't like cats?

f. Who would like a horse?

3. Answer the following questions about Sam's text

a. Where does Sam live?

b. Who is his favourite person?

c. What does his mum do? (2 details)

d. Why does she hate his uncle?

e. Why is his uncle a bad teacher?

4. Fill in the table below

Name	Mariana Pets	Christophe Jobs
Age		
City		
Pets/Job		
Description of pets/job		

Unit 8. Saying what jobs people do: TRANSLATION

1. Faulty translation: spot and correct (in the English) any translation mistakes you find

a. Mon père travaille comme acteur et il aime cela car c'est émouvant. Il travaille dans un théâtre.

My father works as a cook and he really likes his job because it is interesting. He works in a school.

b. Ma tante travaille comme femme d'affaires dans un bureau. Elle aime cela, mais c'est dur.

My aunt works as a businesswoman in a hair salon. She hates it but it's hard.

c. Mon ami Frank travaille comme infirmier. Il travaille dans un hôpital et il aime ça.

My enemy Frank works as a nurse. He lives in a hospital and likes his work.

d. Mon oncle Jean-François est cuisinier dans un restaurant italien et il adore ça.

My uncle Jean-François is a lawyer in an Italian restroom and he likes it.

e. Ma mère Angèle est comptable et elle travaille dans un bureau. Elle déteste son travail, car c'est répétitif et ennuyeux.

My mother Angèle is an actress and works in an office. She loves her work because it is boring and repetitive.

3. Phrase-level translation En to Fr

a. My big brother:

b. Works as:

c. A farmer:

d. He likes:

e. His job:

f. Because it's active:

g. And fun:

2. Translate into English

a. Mon oncle travaille comme:

b. Mon père ne travaille pas:

c. Homme au foyer:

d. Infirmière:

e. Coiffeur:

f. Mécanicien:

g. Elle adore son travail:

h. Il travaille dans un bureau:

i. Elle travaille dans un théâtre:

j. Il travaille dans un garage:

k. C'est gratifiant:

l. C'est dur, mais amusant:

m. Il travaille comme avocat:

4. Sentence-level translation En to Fr

a. My brother is a mechanic.

b. My father is a businessman.

c. My uncle is a farmer and hates his job.

d. My brother Darren works in a restaurant.

e. At home, I have a snake called Serpentine.

f. At home, I have a nice dog and a mean cat.

g. My aunt is a nurse. She likes her job…

h. …because it is rewarding.

i. My aunt works in a hospital.

Unit 8. Saying what jobs people do: WRITING

1. Split sentences

Mon frère a	stimulant
Ma tante est	comme avocat
Mon cousin travaille	professeure
Il aime	dans un restaurant
Car c'est	entreprise
Elle travaille	son travail
Il travaille dans une	un canard noir

2. Rewrite the sentences in the correct order

a. Elle son travail aime beaucoup.

b. travaille dans un comptable Elle comme bureau.

c. Il et homme au foyer est aime ça il.

d. comme oncle fermier Mon travaille.

e. travaille Mon frère un théâtre dans.

f. Mon déteste son grand-père travail.

g. Mon est médecin ami et dans un travaille hôpital.

3. Spot and correct the errors

a. Ma mère est homme au foyer.

b. C'est une travail difficile et ennuyeux.

c. Ma sœur travaille comme coiffeur.

d. Elle déteste son travail car c'est dure et répétitif.

e. Elle travaille dans une hôpital en ville.

f. Elle aime beaucoup son travail car c'est facil.

g. Mon perè déteste son travail.

h. Il aime son travail car c'est gratifiants.

4. Anagrams

a. Micédne:

b. Gratantif:

c. Ritipétéf:

d. Il emai:

e. meeFr:

f. taurRsante:

g. Psorruefes:

5. Guided writing: write 3 short paragraphs describing the people below using the details in the box in 1st person

Person	Relation	Job	Like/ Dislike	Reason
Georges	My dad	Mechanic	Loves	Active and interesting
Lucien	My brother	Lawyer	Hates	Boring and repetitive
Martine	My aunt	Farmer	Likes	Tough but fun

6. Describe this person in French in the 3rd person:

Name: Madeleine

Hair: blond + green eyes

Physique: tall and slim

Personality: hard-working

Job: nurse

Opinion: likes her job a lot

Reason: interesting and rewarding

Grammar Time 4: The present indicative of "Travailler" and other ER verbs

je	**travaille** *I work*		**avocat(e)** *lawyer*
tu	**travailles** *you work*		**coiffeur/euse** *hairdresser*
il mon frère mon père	**travaille** *he works*		**comptable** *accountant* **cuisinier/ère** *chef* **fermier/ère** *farmer*
elle ma sœur ma mère	**travaille** *she works*	**comme** (as)	**homme/femme au foyer** *househusband/wife* **homme/femme d'affaires** *businessman/woman*
nous mon père et moi toi et moi	**travaillons** *we work*		**infirmier/ère** *nurse* **ingénieur(e)** *engineer* **mécanicien/enne** *mechanic*
vous	**travaillez** *you guys work*		**médecin** *doctor*
ils, elles mes frères mes sœurs	**travaillent** *they work*		**plombier/ère** *plumber* **professeur(e)** *teacher* **vendeur/euse** *shop assistant*

Drills

1. Match up

Elle travaille	I work
Je travaille	You work
Ils travaillent	She works
Vous travaillez	We work
Nous travaillons	You guys work
Tu travailles	They work

2. Translate into English

a. Je travaille de temps en temps.

b. Mes parents travaillent beaucoup.

c. Mon frère et moi ne travaillons pas.

d. Elle ne travaille jamais.

e. Tu travailles comme pompier?

f. Vous travaillez dans un magasin?

3. Complete with the correct option

a. Mon frère _____ comme coiffeur.

b. Mes parents ne _____ pas.

c. Mon frère et moi ne _____ pas.

d. Ma petite amie _____ comme hôtesse de l'air.

e. Mes grands-parents ne _____ plus.

f. _____-vous comme policier?

g. Pourquoi tu ne _____ pas?

h. Je ne _____ pas encore

travaillons	travaille	travaillent	travailles
travaillent	travaille	travaillez	travaille

4. Cross out the wrong option

	A	B
Mes parents	travaillent	travaillez
Mon frère	travailles	travaille
Mon père	travaille	travaillent
Mes oncles	travaillez	travaillent
Mes tantes	travaillent	travaillons
Toi et moi	travaillons	travaillez
Nous	travaillent	travaillons
Vous	travaille	travaillez
Mes cousins	travaillent	travaillez
Elle et moi	travaillons	travaillent

5. Complete the verbs

a. Mon frère et moi ne travaill___ ___ ___ pas.

b. Mes parents ne travaill___ ___ ___ pas.

c. Mon père travaill___ comme avocat.

d. Mes frères ne travaill___ ___ ___ pas.

e. Tu ne travaill___ ___ jamais!

f. Ma mère travaill___ à la maison.

g. Mes oncles travaill___ ___ ___ comme cuisiniers.

h. Ma petite amie travaill___ dans une boutique.

i. Vous ne travaill___ ___ jamais!

6. Complete with the correct form of TRAVAILLER

a. Mes parents _____ comme ouvriers: *My parents work as workers*

b. Ma mère _____ comme professeure: *My mother works as a teacher*

c. Mes parents _____ comme comptables: *My parents work as accountants*

d. Mon père _____ comme journaliste: *My father works as a journalist*

e. Mon frère ne _____ pas: *My brother doesn't work*

f. Mes sœurs ne _____ pas non plus: *My sisters don't work either*

g. Mon oncle _____ comme pompier: *My uncle works as a fireman*

h. Mes cousins et moi ne _____ pas: *My cousins and I don't work*

i. Je _____ dans un restaurant: *I work in a restaurant*

j. Ma petite amie _____ dans une boutique: *My girlfriend works in a store*

k. Où _____ -tu ? *Where do you work?*

Verbs like TRAVAILLER

Adorer: to love

Aimer: to like

Déjeuner: to have lunch

Dîner: to have dinner

Écouter: to listen to

Étudier: to study

Jouer: to play

Manger: to eat

Parler: to speak

Regarder: to watch

7. Complete the sentences using the correct form of the verbs in the box on the left

a. J'ador___ mes grands-parents: *I love my grandparents*

b. Elles mang___ des céréales: *They eat cereals*

c. Elle aim___ skier: *She likes skiing*

d. Tu parl___ français? *Do you speak French?*

e. Où dîn___ -tu ? *Where do you have dinner?*

f. Vous jou___ de la guitare? *Do you guys play the guitar?*

g. J'écout___ du rock: *I listen to rock music*

h. Je n'étudi___ jamais: *I never study*

 **THE LANGUAGE GYM**

61

Present Indicative of 'ÊTRE'		Jobs (nouns)	
		Singular	Plural
MASCULINE			
je	suis *I am*	avocat	avocats
		coiffeur	coiffeurs
tu	es *you are*	comptable	comptables
il		cuisinier	cuisiniers
mon frère	est *he is*	fermier	fermiers
mon père		homme au foyer	hommes au foyer
nous	sommes *we are*	homme d'affaires	hommes d'affaires
mon père et moi		infirmier	infirmiers
vous	êtes *you guys are*	ingénieur	ingénieurs
		mécanicien	mécaniciens
ils		médecin	médecins
mes frères	sont *they are*	plombier	plombiers
mes parents		professeur	professeurs
		vendeur	vendeurs
FEMININE			
je	suis *I am*	avocate	avocates
		coiffeuse	coiffeuses
tu	es *you are*	comptable	comptables
elle		cuisinière	cuisinières
ma sœur	est *she is*	fermière	fermières
ma mère		femme au foyer	femmes au foyer
nous (fem)	sommes *we are*	femme d'affaires	femmes d'affaires
ma mère et moi		infirmière	infirmières
vous (fem)	êtes *you guys are*	ingénieure	ingénieures
		mécanicienne	mécaniciennes
elles		médecin	médecins
mes sœurs	sont *they are*	plombière	plombières
mes tantes		professeure	professeures
		vendeuse	vendeuses

Grammar Time 5: ÊTRE (Part 2)
(Present indicative of "Être" and jobs) Drills

1. Match

Je suis	He is
Nous sommes	You are
Elles sont	We are
Tu es	I am
Il est	They are (fem)
Vous êtes	You guys are

2. Complete with the missing forms of ÊTRE

a. Ma mère et moi _____ médecins.

b. Mes frères _____ ouvriers.

c. Ma sœur _____ infirmière.

d. Mes parents et moi _____ jardiniers.

e. Tu _____ avocat?

f. Je _____ pompier.

g. Ils ne _____ pas policiers.

h. Vous _____ mannequins?

i. Vous _____ acteurs, c'est vrai?

j. Mes oncles _____ des chanteurs connus.

3. Translate into English

a. Nous sommes coiffeurs.

b. Ils sont policiers.

c. Es-tu pompier?

d. Marie est mannequin.

e. Ils sont ouvriers sur un chantier. *(building site)*

f. Je suis policier.

g. Vous êtes infirmières?

h. Nous sommes médecins.

i. Mon père et moi sommes acteurs.

j. Vous êtes professeurs?

4. Translate into French (easier)

a. My father is a doctor.

b. My parents are policemen.

c. My uncle is a lawyer.

d. I am a teacher.

e. My cousins are mechanics.

f. My aunt is a singer.

g. My friend Valentin is an actor.

5. Translate into French (harder)

a. My brother is tall and handsome. He is an actor.

b. My older sister is very intelligent and hard-working. She is a scientist.

c. My younger brother is very sporty and active. He is a farmer.

d. My mother is very strong and hard-working. She is a doctor.

e. My father is very patient, calm and organised. He is an accountant.

UNIT 9
Comparing people's appearance and personality

In this unit you will learn how to say in French:
- More/less ... than
- As ... as
- New adjectives to describe people

You will revisit the following:
- Family members
- Pets
- Describing animals appearance and character

UNIT 9
Comparing people

Elle			affectueux/euse(s) *affectionate*	ma grand-mère
Il			aimable(s) *likeable*	mon grand-père
Ma grand-mère			amusant(e)(s) *funny*	mon amie <u>Anne</u>
Mon grand-père			antipathique(s) *unfriendly*	mon ami <u>Paul</u>
Mon amie <u>Anne</u>			barbant(e)(s) *boring*	mon chat
Mon ami <u>Paul</u>			bavard(e)(s) *talkative*	ma sœur
Mon chat			beau(x)/belle(s)	mon frère
Ma sœur			*good-looking*	mon fils
Mon frère			bruyant(e)(s) *noisy*	ma fille
Mon fils			faible(s) *weak*	ma mère
Ma fille			fort(e)(s) *strong*	ma meilleure amie
Ma mère		**plus** *more*	grand(e)(s) *tall*	mon meilleur ami
Ma meilleure amie			gros/se(s) *fat*	mon père
Mon meilleur ami	**est** *is*		intelligent(e)(s) *intelligent*	mon canard
Mon père		**moins** *less*	jeune(s) *young*	mon chien
Mon canard	**sont** *are*		mince(s) *slim*	ma cousine
Mon chien			moche(s) *ugly*	mon cousin
Ma cousine		**aussi** *as*	paresseux/euse(s) *lazy*	ma tortue
Mon cousin			petit(e)(s) *short*	ma tante
Ma tortue			sérieux/euse(s) *serious*	mon oncle
Ma tante		**que** *than / as*	sportif/ive(s) *sporty*	mes grands-parents
Mon oncle			stupide(s) *stupid*	mes sœurs
Mes grands-parents			sympa *nice*	mes frères
Mes sœurs			tranquille(s) *relaxed*	ma petite amie *gf*
Mes frères			travailleur/euse(s) *hard-working*	mon petit ami *bf*
Ma petite amie *gf*			vieux/vieille(s) *old*	mes parents
Mon petit ami *bf*				mes oncles
Mes parents				moi
Mes oncles				

Unit 9. Comparing people : VOCABULARY BUILDING

1. Complete with the missing words

a. Mon père est plus grand _____ mon frère aîné: *My father is taller than my older brother*

b. Ma mère est _____ bavarde que ma _____ : *My mother is less talkative than my aunt*

c. Mon _____ est plus petit que _____ père: *My grandfather is shorter than my father*

d. Mes cousins sont _____ paresseux que _____ : *My cousins are lazier than us*

e. Mon chien _____ plus _____ que mon _____ : *My dog is more noisy than my cat*

f. Ma tante est _____ belle que _____ mère: *My aunt is less pretty than my mother*

g. Mon _____ est plus _____ que moi: *My brother is more hard-working than me*

h. Mon frère cadet est _____ grand _____ moi: *My younger brother is as tall as me*

i. Mes parents _____ plus _____ que mes oncles:
My parents are more affectionate than my uncles

2. Translate into English

a. Mes cousins

b. Plus

c. Mon oncle

d. Mes grands-parents

e. Ma sœur

f. Mon meilleur ami

g. Travailleur

h. Mon amie

i. Grand

j. Vieux

k. Têtu

l. Paresseux

3. Match French and English

Travailleur	Sporty
Beau	Stupid
Aimable	Strong
Fort	Good-looking
Sportif	Old
Vieux	Hard-working
Bête	Likeable

4. Spot and correct any English translation mistakes

a. Il est plus grand que moi: *He is taller than you*

b. Il est aussi beau que nous: *He is as good-looking as me*

c. Il est plus tranquille que moi: *He is stronger than me*

d. Nous sommes moins gros que lui: *I am fatter than him*

e. Ils sont moins petits que nous: *They are shorter than us*

f. Je suis aussi vieux que lui: *She is as old as him*

g. Il est plus sportif que moi: *You are sportier than me*

5. Complete with a suitable word

a. Ma mère est _____ grande _____ moi.

b. _____ père _____ plus jeune que mon oncle.

c. Mes parents sont _____ grands _____ mes grands-parents.

d. _____ frères _____ plus sportifs que mes cousins.

e. Mon _____ est moins bruyant _____ mon canard.

f. Mes grands-parents _____ aussi aimables _____ mes parents.

g. Ma petite amie est _____ belle qu' _____ tortue.

6. Match the opposites

Beau	Petit
Travailleur	Ennuyeux
Jeune	Moche
Grand	Gros
Amusant	Moins
Faible	Paresseux
Plus	Vieux
Mince	Fort

 **THE LANGUAGE GYM**

Unit 9. Comparing people : READING

Je m'appelle Georges. J'ai vingt ans et j'habite à Bayonne. Dans ma famille nous sommes cinq personnes: mes parents et mes deux frères, Philippe et Alain. Philippe est plus grand, beau et fort qu'Alain, mais Alain est plus aimable, intelligent et travailleur que Philippe.

Mes parents s'appellent Anthony et Ninon. Ils sont tous deux très aimables, mais mon père est plus strict que ma mère. De plus, ma mère est plus patiente et moins têtue que mon père. Moi, je suis aussi têtu que mon père.

À la maison, nous avons deux animaux: une tortue et un canard. Tous deux sont très sympathiques, mais mon canard est plus bruyant. Aussi bruyant que moi…

Je m'appelle Erwan. J'ai quinze ans et je vis à Carnac. Dans ma famille nous sommes cinq: mes parents et mes deux frères, Ronan et Périg. Ronan est plus mince et sportif que Périg, mais Périg est plus grand et très fort.

Mes parents s'appellent Carmen et Anthony. Je préfère mon père car il est moins strict que ma mère. De plus, ma mère est plus têtue que mon père. Je suis aussi têtu qu'elle! Chez nous, nous avons deux animaux: un perroquet et un cochon d'Inde. Tous deux sont très sympathiques, mais mon perroquet est beaucoup plus bavard. Aussi bavard que moi…

Je m'appelle Vinciane. J'ai vingt ans et je vis à Lille avec mes parents et mes deux sœurs, Marina et Véronique. Marina est plus jolie que Véronique, mais Véronique est plus sympathique.

Mes parents sont très chaleureux et aimables, mais mon père est plus amusant que ma mère. De plus, mon père est plus joueur que ma mère. Moi, je suis aussi joueuse que mon père!

À la maison, nous avons deux animaux: un chien et un lapin. Tous deux sont très gros, mais mon chien est plus paresseux. Aussi paresseux que moi…

1. Find the French for the following in Georges' text

a. I live in:

b. My parents:

c. Good-looking:

d. Hard-working:

e. Less stubborn:

f. More patient:

g. But:

h. My duck:

i. Two pets:

j. Very kind:

k. As stubborn as:

l. Strong:

m. Both of them:

2. Complete the statements below based on Vinciane's text

a. I am _____ years old.

b. Marina is more _____ than Véronique.

c. Véronique is more _____.

d. My parents are very _____ and _____.

e. I am as _____ as my father.

f. We have _____ pets.

3. Correct any of the statements below about Erwan's text which are incorrect

a. Erwan a trois animaux.

b. Ronan est moins gros que Périg.

c. Ronan est plus faible que Périg.

d. Erwan est aussi bavard que son cochon d'Inde.

e. Erwan préfère sa mère.

4. Answer the questions on the three texts above

a. Where does Erwan live?

b. Who is stricter, his mother or his father?

c. Who is as talkative as their parrot?

d. Who is as noisy as their duck?

e. Who has a stubborn father?

f. Who has a rabbit?

g. Who has a guinea pig?

h. Which one of Erwan's brothers is sportier?

i. What are the differences between Erwan's brothers?

Unit 9. Comparing people: TRANSLATION/WRITING

1. Translate into English

a. Grand:

b. Mince:

c. Petit:

d. Gros:

e. Intelligent:

f. Têtu:

g. Bête:

h. Beau:

i. Moche:

j. Plus…que:

k. Moins…que:

l. Fort:

m. Faible:

n. Aussi…que:

2. Gapped sentences

a. Ma _____ est _____ grande _____ ma tante:
My mother is taller than my aunt

b. _____ père _____ plus _____ que mon frère aîné:
My father is stronger than my older brother

c. Mes _____ sont moins _____ que nous:
My cousins are less sporty than us

d. _____ frère est _____ bête que _____ :
My brother is more stupid than me

e. Ma mère _____ _____ aimable _____ mon père:
My mother is as kind as my father

f. Ma _____ est _____ travailleuse que _____ :
My sister is more hard-working than us

g. Ma _____ _____ est moins _____ _____ moi:
My girlfriend is less serious than me

h. Mon _____ _____ est _____ têtu _____ ma grand-mère:
My grandfather is more stubborn than my grandmother

3. Phrase-level translation En to Fr

a. My mother is:

b. Taller than:

c. As slim as:

d. Less stubborn than:

e. I am shorter than:

f. My parents are:

g. My cousins are:

h. As fat as:

i. They are as strong as:

j. My grandparents are:

k. I am as lazy as:

4. Sentence-level translation En to Fr

a. My older sister is taller than my younger sister.

b. My father is as stubborn as my mother.

c. My girlfriend is more hard-working than me.

d. I am less intelligent than my brother.

e. My best friend is stronger and sportier than me.

f. My boyfriend is better-looking than me.

g. My cousins are uglier than us.

h. My duck is noisier than my dog.

i. My cat is funnier than my turtle.

j. My rabbit is less fat than my guinea pig.

k. I am taller than you.

Revision Quickie 2 : Family, Pets and Jobs

1. Match

Ouvrier	Doctor
Avocat	Waiter
Infirmier	Journalist
Serveur	Nurse
Journaliste	IT worker
Médecin	Worker
Hôtesse de l'air	Air hostess
Pompier	Lawyer
Informaticien	Firefighter

2. Sort the words listed below in the categories in the table

a. ouvrier; b. grand; c. plombier; d. amusant; e. petit;
f. cousin; g. professeur; h. infirmier; i. oncle; j. père ;
k. bleu; l. gros; m. beau; n. plombier; o. mère; p. frère;
q. lapin; r. châtain; s. canard; t. chat

Description	Animaux	Travail	Famille

3. Complete with the missing adjectives

a. Mon père est _____ *fat*

b. Ma mère est _____ *tall*

c. Mon frère est _____ *short*

d. Ma petite amie est _____ *good-looking*

e. Mon cousin est _____ *annoying*

f. Mon prof d'anglais est _____ *boring*

4. Complete with the missing nouns

a. Mon père travaille comme _____ *lawyer*

b. Ma mère est _____ *nurse*

c. Mon meilleur ami est _____ *journalist*

d. Ma sœur est _____ *air hostess*

e. Mon cousin est _____ *student*

f. Moi je travaille comme _____ *doctor*

g. Martine est _____ *sales assistant*

h. Ma grand-mère est _____ *singer*

5. Match the opposites

Grand	Travailleur
Beau	Stupide
Gros	Petit
Paresseux	Silencieux
Intelligent	Moche
Bruyant	Impatient
Mauvais	Mince
Patient	Bon

6. Complete the numbers below

a. Quato__ __ __ 14

b. Quara__ __ __ 40

c. Soixa__ __ __ 60

d. Cinqu__ __ __ 50

e. Soixante-__ __ __ 70

f. Quatre-vingt-__ __ __ 90

7. Complete with the correct verb

a. Ma mère _____ grande: *My mother is tall*

b. _____ les cheveux noirs: *I have black hair*

c. _____ comme plombier:

I work as a plumber

d. Mon père _____ quarante ans: *My father is 40*

e. Combien de personnes _____ dans ta famille?

How many people are there in your family?

f. Mes frères _____ grands: *My brothers are tall*

g. Ma sœur ne _____ pas:

My sister doesn't work

h. Ma _____ _____ _____ Mariana:

My girlfriend is called Mariana

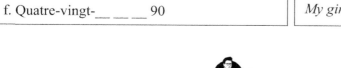

UNIT 10
Saying what's in my school bag / classroom/ describing colour

Grammar Time: Avoir & Agreements

In this unit you will learn how to say:

- What objects you have is in your schoolbag/pencil case/classroom
- Words for classroom equipment
- What you have and don't have

You will revisit the following:

- Colours
- How adjectives agree in gender and number with nouns
- Introducing yourself (e.g. name, age, town, country)
- Pets

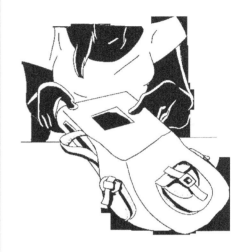

BONJOUR!

UNIT 10.
Saying what's in my school bag/classroom/describing colour

Dans ma trousse *in my pencilcase*	Dans ma classe *in my class*		
		MASC	noir
Il y a / Il n'y a pas de/d'	**un agenda** *a planner*		blanc
There is / There isn't	**un cahier** *an exercise book*		jaune
	un crayon *a pencil*		
	un dictionaire *a dictionary*		rouge
J'ai / Je n'ai pas de/d'	**un feutre** *a felt tip pen*		bleu
I have / I don't have	**un livre** *a book*		vert
	un ordinateur *a computer*		
	un stylo *a pen*		gris
J'ai besoin de/d'	**un stylo à plume** *a fountain pen*		rose
I need	**un taille-crayon** *a pencil sharpener*		orange
	un tube de colle *a gluestick*		
		MASC PLURAL	jaunes
Je n'ai pas besoin de/d'	**des ciseaux** *scissors*		bleus
I don't need	**des crayons** *some pencils*		rouges
	des feutres *some felt tip pens*		verts
Mon ami Denis a	**des stylos** *some pens*		
My friend Denis has			
	une calculatrice *a calculator*	**FEM**	noire
	une chaise *a chair*		blanche
Mon ami Denis n'a pas de	**une gomme** *a rubber*		bleue
My friend Denis does not have	**une règle** *a ruler*		verte
	une table *a table*		grise
		FEM PLURAL	
	des trousses *some pencil cases*		vertes

Author's note: *in the negative form in French the "un/une" or "des" turns into "de" or d'*
Examples: Je n'ai pas de calculatrice *(I don't have a calculator)*
Notice the "d'" in front of a vowel ex: -Je n'ai pas besoin d'agenda *(I don't need a planner)*
-Il n'y a pas d'ordinateur *(There isn't a computer)*

 **THE LANGUAGE GYM**

Unit 10. Saying what's in my school bag: VOCABULARY BUILDING

1. Complete with the missing word

a. Dans mon sac, j'ai un _____ :
In my bag, I have an exercise book

b. J'ai besoin d'une _____ : *I need an eraser*

c. Je n'ai pas ____ stylo: *I don't have a pen*

d. Mon ami ___ un livre: *My friend has a book*

e. J'ai _____ calculatrice: *I have a calculator*

f. J'ai besoin d'une _____ : *I need a chair*

g. Je n'ai pas de _____ : *I don't have a ruler*

h. Mon ami n'a pas de _____ :
My friend doesn't have any scissors

2. Match up

une gomme	a pencil
un crayon	a planner
un agenda	I have a
une chaise	a sharpener
j'ai un	a pen
j'ai besoin de	I don't have a
je n'ai pas de	a chair
un taille-crayon	an eraser
un stylo	I need

3. Translate into English

a. J'ai une gomme.

b. Mon ami a un agenda.

c. Je n'ai pas de cahier.

d. J'ai un crayon vert.

e. Je n'ai pas de taille-crayon.

f. J'ai besoin d'un feutre.

g. Il y a un ordinateur.

h. Je n'ai pas de feutre.

4. Add the missing letter

a. Un t__ille-crayon

b. Une g__mme

c. J'ai b__soin

d. Je n'ai pas d_

e. Un __genda

f. Mon am___

g. Il n'__ pas de

h. Un ta__leau

5. Anagrams

a. onCray = Crayon

b. essTrou =

c. geOanr =

d. Blcan =

e. eauxsiC =

f. caS =

g. genAda =

h. rtVe =

6. Broken words

a. D__ns m____ s_____ j'_____ u___ t_____
In my bag I have a pencil case

b. Dan__ m_____ t_____ j'_____ d___
c_____ *In my pencil case I have some pencils*

c. J___ n'_____ p_____ de g_____
I don't have an eraser

d. __'ai b_____ d'_____ r_____
I need a ruler

e. Il __ a u__ t_____ b_____
There is a whiteboard

f. J'___ d___ s_____ b_____
I have some blue pens

7. Complete with a suitable word

a. J'ai un _____

b. J'ai _____ d'un crayon

c. J'aime la couleur _____

d. _____ un ordinateur

e. Un tableau _____

f. Une _____ rouge

g. Mon _____ a une trousse

h. _____ une règle

i. Mon ami n' ____ pas de feutre

j. Un stylo _____

k. Il y a un _____ blanc

Unit 10. Saying what's in my school bag: READING

Je m'appelle Renée. J'ai douze ans et je vis à Rome, en Italie. Dans ma famille il y a quatre personnes. J'ai un chat blanc. Dans mon sac, j'ai beaucoup de choses: un stylo rouge, un crayon jaune, une règle rose et une gomme blanche. Mon amie Lucie a seulement une chose dans sa trousse, un crayon. Mais chez elle, elle a un cheval gris!

Je m'appelle Andréa. J'ai quinze ans et je vis à Paris, en France. Dans ma famille, il y a trois personnes. J'ai un lapin très amusant. Dans ma classe, il y a beaucoup de choses. Il y a un tableau blanc, un ordinateur et trente tables. Ma classe est très grande. J'ai un crayon bleu, un feutre jaune, une règle neuve et une gomme. Mon ami Martin a des crayons de toutes les couleurs.

Je m'appelle Lucas. J'ai dix-huit ans et je suis de Cadix, en Espagne. Dans ma famille, il y a cinq personnes. Mon frère s'appelle Andy. Dans ma classe, il y a un tableau blanc et vingt tables. Il y a aussi vingt chaises. Une pour chaque personne. Ma classe est jolie et mon professeur est très amusant. Mais, je n'ai pas de feutres, ni de crayons, ni de règle, ni de gomme. Je n'ai rien. J'ai besoin de tout en fait. Chez moi, j'ai une très jolie souris blanche.

Je m'_____ Léo. J'ai huit a___ et je ____ à Étretat, en France. Dans ma famille _____ quatre personnes. Dans ma _____ il y a beaucoup de choses, comme ____ ordinateur et un t_____ b_____. Dans ma _____, j'ai une r_____, un crayon b_____ et une g_____. Mon ami a beaucoup de c_____, mais il n'a pas de g_____.

Je m'appelle Émilien. J'ai onze ans et je vis à Bruges, une ville en Belgique. Dans ma famille il y a quatre personnes. J'adore ma mère, mais je n'aime pas mon père. Il est toujours méchant. Il est avocat. Dans ma classe, il n'y a pas beaucoup de choses. Il n'y a pas de tableau ni d'ordinateur. Il y a vingt-trois tables, mais seulement vingt-deux chaises. C'est un problème! J'ai une calculatrice, un crayon et un agenda.

1. Find the French for the following in Renée's text

a. I am 12

b. I live in Rome

c. There are 4 people

d. A white cat

e. A red pencil

f. A yellow pencil

g. In her pencil case

h. Only has one thing

i. In her house

j. A grey horse

2. Find Someone Who

a. …has a blue pencil

b. …has most tables in their class

c. …has a class with one student always standing

d. …has no school equipment

e. …has a big pet

f. …doesn't like their dad

3. Answer the following questions about Lucas' text

a. Where does Lucas live?

b. Who is Andy?

c. How many tables and chairs in his class?

d. How does he describe his class?

e. What school equipment does he have?

f. What pet does he have?

g. How does he describe his pet?

4. Fill in the table below

Name	Renée	Andréa
Age		
City		
Items in pencil case		

Unit 10. Saying what's in my school bag: TRANSLATION

1. Faulty translation: spot and correct (in the English) any translation mistakes you find below

a. Dans ma classe, il y a deux tableaux blancs et un ordinateur. Je n'aime pas mon professeur.
In my class, there is a whiteboard and a computer. I like my teacher.

b. Je n'ai pas beaucoup de choses dans ma trousse. J'ai un crayon rose, mais je n'ai pas de règle.
I have many things in my pencil case. I have a red pencil, but I don't have an eraser.

c. Mon ami Émilien a quatre personnes dans sa famille. Il a besoin d'un feutre noir et d'un agenda.
My friend Émilien has five people in his family. He needs a black pen and a diary.

d. J'ai besoin d'un taille-crayon et d'un tube de colle. Je n'ai pas de règle ou de crayon. J'adore ma professeure!
I need paper and a rubber. I don't have a ruler or a pencil. I hate my teacher!

e. Dans ma classe, il y a trente tables et trente chaises. J'ai besoin d'un agenda, mais j'ai un dictionnaire.
In my class there are thirty cats and thirty chairs. I need a calculator, but I have a dictionary.

3. Phrase-level translation En to Fr

a. A red book:

b. A black calculator:

c. I don't have:

d. I need:

e. I like:

f. There are:

g. I have:

h. My friend has:

2. Translate into English

a. J'ai besoin d'une gomme:

b. J'ai un stylo noir:

c. J'ai un crayon bleu:

d. Une règle verte:

e. J'ai un chien chez moi:

f. Mon ami a un livre:

g. Mon père travaille comme:

h. J'aime mon professeur:

i. Des crayons jaunes:

j. Un grand tableau blanc:

k. J'ai beaucoup de choses:

l. Je n'ai pas de taille-crayon:

m. J'ai besoin d'un dictionnaire:

4. Sentence-level translation En to Fr

a. There are twenty tables.

b. There is a whiteboard.

c. My teacher is nice.

d. I have some blue pens.

e. I have some orange pencils.

f. I need an eraser and a sharpener.

g. I need a chair and a book.

h. My class is very big and pretty.

i. My father is a teacher.

THE LANGUAGE GYM

Unit 10. Saying what's in my school bag: WRITING

1. Split sentences

J'ai une	stylo à plume
J'ai besoin	pas mon oncle
Ma classe	d'un crayon
Il y a trente	calculatrice
Mon ami n'a pas de	est grande
Je n'aime	un stylo rouge
J'ai	tables

2. Rewrite the sentences in the correct order

a. J'ai d' besoin calculatrice une.

b. J'ai une règle rouge un crayon et noir.

c. Ma très grande classe est.

d. Mon ami livre blanc a un.

e. Je bleu n'ai d'agenda pas.

f. J'ai moi tortue une verte chez.

g. Mon est médecin père et dans un travaille hôpital il.

3. Spot and correct the grammar and spelling note: in several cases a word is missing

a. Dans ma classe il y a vingt table.

b. J'ai un calculatrice noire.

c. Dans ma trousse j'a beaucoup choses.

d. Mon ami n'ai rien dans sa trousses.

e. J'i besoin d'un crayon grise et d'un gomme.

f. Mon ami Fernand a crayons de toutes les couleurs.

g. Ma mere est mécanicien et travaille dans un garage.

h. Je suis grand et fort. J'ai les cheveux blondes et les yeux bleu.

4. Anagrams

a. sestrou = trousse

b. velir =

c. yoncra =

d. momge =

e. erteuf =

f. elilta-onyarc =

g. prsorusfe =

6. Describe this person in French:

Name: Denis

Pet: a black horse

Hair: brown + blue eyes

School equipment: has pen, pencil, ruler, eraser

Does not have: sharpener, paper, chair

Favourite colour: blue

5. Guided writing: write 3 short paragraphs describing these people's school bags using the details in the box

Person	Lives	Has	Hasn't	Needs
Nathalie	Paris	Exercise book	Pen	Diary
Irène	Bordeaux	Ruler	Pencil	A paper
Juliette	Valence	Felt tip	Sharpener	A gluestick

Grammar Time 6: AVOIR (Part 3) + AGREEMENTS
Present indicative of "Avoir" (to have) and agreement training

j'ai *I have*	**deux grands-pères, deux grands-mères**
tu as *you have*	**un frère, une sœur**
il/elle a *he/she has*	**deux frères, deux sœurs**
nous avons *we have*	**un fils, une fille**
vous avez *you guys have*	**un petit ami, une petite amie**
ils/elles ont *they have*	**un cousin, une cousine**
	un oncle, une tante

un cahier	**douze ans**
une calculatrice	**treize ans**
un stylo	**quatorze ans**
un crayon	**quinze ans**
un dictionnaire	**seize ans**
un feutre	**dix-sept ans**
un livre	**dix-huit ans**
un ordinateur	**dix-neuf ans**
un stylo à plume	**vingt ans**
une trousse	**(Here 'avoir' = 'to be' in English)**

cours de dessin à huit heures	**un canard**
cours de sciences à neuf heures	**un chat**
cours d'espagnol à dix heures	**un cheval**
cours de français à onze heures	**un chien**
cours de géographie à midi	**un hamster**
cours d'histoire à une heure	**un lapin**
cours de mathématiques à deux heures	**un oiseau**
cours d'éducation physique à trois heures	**un perroquet**
de très bons professeurs	**un poisson**
de très mauvais professeurs	**une souris**

Present indicative of "Avoir" (to have) in the negative form

je n'ai pas de *I don't have*	**nous n'avons pas de** *we haven't*
tu n'as pas de *you don't have*	**vous n'avez pas de** *you guys don't have*
il/elle n'a pas de *he/she doesn't have*	**ils/elles n'ont pas de** *they don't have*

cahier calculatrice crayon crayon de couleur dictionnaire feutre livre (d') ordinateur stylo à plume trousse	grand-père, grand-mère frère, sœur fils, fille petit ami, petite amie cousin, cousine (d') oncle, tante
cours de dessin à huit heures cours de sciences à neuf heures cours d'espagnol à dix heures cours de français à onze heures cours de géographie à midi cours d'histoire à une heure cours de mathématiques à deux heures cours d'éducation physique à trois heures bons professeurs mauvais professeurs	canard chat cheval chien hamster lapin (d') oiseau perroquet poisson souris

*je n'ai pas	douze ans treize ans quatorze ans quinze ans seize ans	dix-sept ans dix-huit ans dix-neuf ans vingt ans

*Author's note: when talking about age in the negative, e.g. saying "I am not 12" there is no "de", unlike the rest of the boxes above. Don't forget, in French you use "avoir" to say how old you are, therefore "je n'ai pas douze ans" literally means you "I don't have 12 years".

Present indicative of "Avoir" + Agreements: Verb drills (1)

1. Match up

J'ai	We have
Nous avons	I have
Tu as	They have
Il/elle a	You have
Vous avez	He/she has
Ils ont	You guys have

2. Complete with the missing words (Pets/family members)

a. Je _____ d'animaux *I don't have pets*

b. _____ un chat gris *We have a grey cat*

c. _____ deux tortues *They have two turtles*

d. _____ des frères ou des sœurs? *Do you have siblings?*

e. _____ animaux? *Do you guys have pets?*

f. Mon frère _____ un cochon d'Inde *My brother has a guinea pig*

g. Mon cousin n' _____ d'animaux *My cousin doesn't have pets*

h. Mes cousins n' _____ animaux *My cousins have no pets*

3. Complete with the present indicative form of "avoir"

J'____

Tu ____

Il, elle, on ____

Nous _____

Vous _____

Ils/elles _____

4. Add in the correct verb form

a. Mon oncle n'____ pas d'animaux.

b. Mes oncles _____ deux chiens.

c. Maintenant j'____ cours d'histoire.

d. À midi, nous _____ géographie.

e. Mon frère _____ dix ans.

f. Mes parents _____ quarante ans.

g. Mon père _____ les cheveux blancs.

h. Mes sœurs _____ les cheveux roux.

5. Complete with an appropriate word

a. Mon _____ a quarante ans.

b. Ma mère ____ trente-deux ans.

c. Mes parents ____ les yeux bleus, mais moi _____ les yeux noirs.

d. Mon oncle n'a pas d' _____ .

e. Tu ____ des frères et des sœurs?

f. Vous _____ de très beaux cheveux.

g. Je _____ d'animaux, mais mon _____ a un cochon d'Inde.

6. Translate into French

a. My father has blue eyes.

b. I don't have pets.

c. I don't have a pen.

d. In my pencil case I have a ruler.

e. Do you have any felt-tip pens?

f. I have a dog at home.

g. My mother is 40.

h. My father is 38.

i. Do you guys have history today?

j. How old are you?

Present indicative of "Avoir" + Agreements
Verb drills (2)

7. Translate the pronoun and verb into French as shown in the example

I have: **J'ai**

You have:

She has:

He has:

We have:

You guys have:

They (F) have:

They (M) have:

8. Translate into French. Topic: Pets and colours

a. We have a blue parrot.

b. I have two green turtles.

c. My brother has a white guinea pig.

d. My uncles have a black horse.

e. My sister has a red and black spider.

f. We don't have pets at home.

g. Do you have pets at home?

9. Translate into French. Topic: family members

a. I don't have any brothers:

b. We have two grandparents:

c. My mother has no sisters:

d. Do you have any brothers or sisters?

e. Do you guys have cousins?

f. He doesn't have any pets:

10. Translate into French. Topic: Age

a. They are fifteen years old:

b. We are fourteen years old:

c. I am sixteen years old:

d. You guys are twelve years old:

e. How old are you?

f. My mother is forty:

11. Translate into French. Topic: Hair and eyes

a. I have black hair.

b. We have blue eyes.

c. She has curly hair.

d. My mother has blonde hair.

e. Do you have grey eyes?

f. They have green eyes.

g. My brother has brown eyes.

h. We have no hair.

i. You guys have beautiful eyes.

j. My parents have red hair.

k. You have no hair.

l. My sister has very long hair.

Grammar Time 7: Agreements (Part 1)

1. Complete the table

English	Français
Yellow	
	Rose
	Gris
Green	
Red	
	Violet
	Bleu
Noir	
	Blanc
Blue	

2. Translate into English

a. Un crayon jaune:

b. Une trousse noire:

c. Des cahiers roses:

d. Des feutres rouges:

e. Un stylo à plume bleu:

f. Deux stylos bleus:

g. Un sac orange:

h. Un taille-crayon gris:

i. Un stylo à plume rouge:

j. Un sac jaune et rouge:

3. Provide the feminine version of each adjective

Masculin	Féminin
jaune	
vert	
bleu	
rouge	
blanc	
noir	
orange	

4. Complete with the missing adjective

a. J'ai un sac _____ *I have a red schoolbag*

b. J'ai un stylo _____ *I have a black pen*

c. J'ai un stylo à plume _____ *I have a blue fountain pen*

d. J'ai une règle _____ *I have a yellow ruler*

e. J'ai une feuille _____ *I have a white sheet of paper*

f. J'ai des ciseaux _____ *I have green scissors*

g. J'ai des feutres _____ *I have blue felt tip pens*

h. J'ai un sac _____ *I have a black schoolbag*

5. Translate into French

a. A red fountain pen:

b. A black ruler:

c. A green bag:

d. A yellow pencil case:

e. Two green rulers:

f. Two blue scissors:

g. Two pink exercise books:

6. Translate into French

a. I have a red pen and a blue fountain pen.

b. Philippe has a green schoolbag.

c. Do you have a white pencil case?

d. Do you guys have any red felt tip pens?

e. I have a pink sheet of paper.

f. We have a yellow bag.

g. He has a black and white ruler.

UNIT 11 (Part 1)
Talking about food:
Likes/dislikes and why

Grammar Time: Manger /Boire

In this unit will learn how to say:

- What food you like/dislike and to what extent
- Why you like/dislike it (old and new expressions)
- New adjectives
- The full conjugation of 'manger' *to eat* and 'boire' *to drink*

You will revisit the following
- Time markers
- Providing a justification

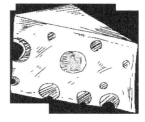

UNIT 11: Talking about food
Likes/dislikes and why Part 1

J'adore *I love* **J'aime beaucoup** *I like a lot* **J'aime** *I like* **J'aime un peu** *I like a bit*	**le café** *coffee* **le chocolat** *chocolate* **le fromage** *cheese* **le jus de fruits** *fruit juice* **le lait** *milk* **le miel** *honey* **le pain** *bread* **le poisson** *fish* **le poulet rôti** *roast chicken* **le riz** *rice* **la salade verte** *green salad* **la viande** *meat* **l'eau** *water* (l' + vowel)	***parce que c'est** *because it is*	**dégoûtant** *disgusting* **délicieux** *delicious* **dur** *hard* **épicé** *spicy* **gras** *greasy* **juteux** *juicy* **malsain** *unhealthy* **rafraîchissant** *refreshing* **sain** *healthy* **savoureux** *tasty* **sucré** *sweet*
Je n'aime pas *I don't like* **Je déteste** *I hate* **Je préfère** *I prefer*	**les chocolats** *chocolates* **les fruits** *fruit* **les hamburgers** *burgers* **les légumes** *vegetables* **les œufs** *eggs*	**parce qu'ils sont** *because they are*	**dégoûtant(e)s** *disgusting* **délicieux/euses** *delicious* **dur(e)s** *hard* **épicé(e)s** *spicy* **gras(se)s** *greasy* **juteux/euses** *juicy* **malsain(e)s** *unhealthy* **rafraîchissant(e)s** *refreshing* **sain(e)s** *healthy* **savoureux/euses** *tasty* **sucré(e)s** *sweet*
	les bananes *bananas* **les fraises** *strawberries* **les crevettes** *prawns* **les oranges** *oranges* **les pommes** *apples* **les tomates** *tomatoes*	****parce qu'elles sont** *because they are*	

PLEASE NOTE

* After "c'est" an adjective is always in its masculine singular form

E.g. J'aime la viande, c'est délicieux.

** However, in the second section after "ils sont" or "elles sont", adjectives agree both in gender and number

E.g. J'aime les œufs parce qu'ils sont sains.

E.g. J'aime les tomates parce qu'elles sont saines.

Unit 11. Talking about food (Part 1): VOCABULARY BUILDING (Part 1)

1. Match up

Les bananes	Eggs
Les fraises	Apples
La viande	Prawns
Le poulet	Milk
L'eau	Fruit
Le lait	Water
Les œufs	Burgers
Les crevettes	Chicken
Les hamburgers	Meat
Les fruits	Bananas
Les pommes	Strawberries

2. Complete

a. J'aime beaucoup le _____ *I like chicken a lot*

b. J'adore les _____ *I love prawns*

c. J'aime les _____ *I like strawberries*

d. J'adore le _____ *I love milk*

e. J'adore les _____ *I love bananas*

f. Je préfère l' ____ minérale *I prefer mineral water*

g. Je n'aime pas les _____ *I don't like tomatoes*

h. Je déteste le _____ *I hate chicken*

i. J'adore les _____ *I love fruit*

j. Je n'aime pas les _____ *I don't like eggs*

k. Je préfère les _____ *I prefer vegetables*

3. Translate into English

a. J'aime les fruits

b. Je déteste les œufs

c. J'adore le poulet rôti

d. J'aime les hamburgers

e. Je déteste la viande

f. Je préfère les oranges

g. Je n'aime pas les tomates

h. Je déteste le lait

4. Complete the words

a. Le fro_____

b. Les ba_____

c. Les fr_____

d. Les lég_____

e. Les hamb_____

f. Les cre_____

g. Le poi_____

h. Le r____

5. Turn the negative opinions into positive ones and vice versa

a. Je déteste les pâtes: J'adore les pâtes

b. Je n'aime pas les légumes: J'aime les légumes

c. J'adore les fruits:

d. Je n'aime pas le lait:

e. J'aime le poisson:

f. Je déteste le pain:

g. Je déteste le chocolat:

h. J'adore les fraises:

i. Je n'aime pas le café:

6. Translate into French

a. I like eggs:

b. I love oranges:

c. I hate tomatoes:

d. I don't like prawns:

e. I love fruit:

f. I don't like vegetables:

g. I hate milk:

Unit 11. Talking about food (Part 1): VOCABULARY BUILDING (Part 2)

1. Complete with the missing words. The initial letter of each word is given

a. Ces bananes sont d_____
These bananas are disgusting

b. Ces pommes sont d_____
These apples are delicious

c. Ce poulet est très é_____
This chicken is very spicy

d. Je n'aime pas la v_____
I don't like meat

e. Ce café est très s_____
This coffee is very sweet

f. Les hamburgers sont m_____
Burgers are unhealthy

g. Les légumes sont s_____
Vegetables are healthy

h. Ce jus de fruits est r_____
This fruit juice is refreshing

i. Ces fraises sont j_____
These strawberries are juicy

2. Complete the table

Français	English
Le lait	
	Roast chicken
Le poisson	
Les œufs	
	Honey
Le pain	
Les céréales	
Le pain grillé	
	Prawns
	Vegetables
L'eau	

3. Broken words

a. J__ n'_____ p___ l___ o_____ *I don't like eggs*

b. J'_____ l__ p_____ *I love apples*

c. Je d_____ l___ h_____
I hate burgers

d. J'_____ b_____ p l__ c_____
I like chocolates a lot

e. L__ c_____ c'est s_____
Coffee is tasty

f. L__ p_____ c'_____ s_____
Fish is healthy

g. L__ curry indien c'_____ t_____ é_____
Indian curry is very spicy

h. L'_____, c'est r_____
Water is refreshing

4. Complete each sentence in a way which is logical and grammatically correct

a. Les _____ ne sont pas saines.

b. Les bananes sont _____.

c. Je n' _____ pas le lait.

d. J' _____ le poulet rôti.

e. _____ le poisson car c'est délicieux.

f. _____ la viande rouge car c'est malsain.

g. _____ les légumes car c'est sain et délicieux.

h. Je_____ le fromage car c'est dégoûtant.

Unit 11. Talking about food (Part 1): READING

Bonjour! Je m'appelle Robert. Qu'est-ce que je préfère manger? J'adore les fruits de mer, donc j'aime beaucoup les crevettes et les calamars car ils sont délicieux. J'aime beaucoup le poisson aussi, car c'est savoureux et riche en protéines. Surtout le saumon. J'aime assez le poulet rôti. De plus, j'aime les fruits, surtout les bananes et les fraises. Je n'aime pas les légumes car ils ne sont pas savoureux.

Salut! Je m'appelle Alexandre. Qu'est-ce que je préfère manger? J'adore les légumes. J'en mange tous les jours. Mes légumes préférés sont les épinards, les carottes et les aubergines car ils sont riches en vitamines et minéraux. J'aime aussi les fruits car ils sont sains et délicieux. Je déteste la viande et le poisson. Ils sont riches en protéines, mais ne sont pas savoureux.

Bonjour! Je m'appelle Violette. Qu'est-ce que je préfère manger? J'adore la viande, surtout la viande d'agneau, car c'est très savoureux. J'aime beaucoup le poulet rôti épicé car c'est délicieux et riche en protéines. J'aime assez les œufs. Ils sont sains et riches en vitamines et protéines. J'aime assez les fruits, surtout les cerises. Elles sont délicieuses et juteuses. Je n'aime pas du tout les pommes.

Bonjour! Je m'appelle Xavier. Qu'est-ce que je préfère manger? Je préfère la viande. J'adore ça car c'est savoureux. J'aime beaucoup les hamburgers car ils sont délicieux. J'aime aussi beaucoup les fruits car ils sont sucrés. Je n'aime pas les légumes. Je déteste les tomates et les carottes. Je ne supporte pas les œufs. Ils sont riches en vitamines et protéines, mais ils sont dégoûtants. Je n'aime pas les frites car elles sont malsaines.

Salut! Je m'appelle Fernand. Qu'est-ce que je préfère manger? J'adore la viande rouge parce que c'est très savoureux et riche en protéines. Je ne mange pas beaucoup de poisson car je n'aime pas cela. J'aime assez les frites, mais elles ne sont pas saines. J'adore les fruits, surtout les bananes, car elles sont délicieuses, riches en vitamines et pas chères. Je n'aime pas les pommes et je déteste les oranges. Je ne mange pas de légumes.

1. Find the French for the following in Robert's text

a. I love seafood

b. I like prawns a lot

c. They are delicious

d. Fish also

e. Salmon

f. I quite like

g. Moreover

h. Above all

i. They are not tasty

2. Violette, Fernand or Robert? Write V, F or R next to each statement

a. I love seafood - *Robert*

b. I hate oranges

c. Especially cherries

d. I don't like vegetables

e. I prefer salmon

f. I quite like fries

g. I love meat (lamb)

h. I don't eat much fish

3. Complete the following sentences based on Alexandre's text

a. Alexandre loves_____

b. He eats them _____

c. His favourite vegetables are _____,
_____ and _____

d. He also likes _____ because it is
_____ and _____

e. He hates _____ and _____

4. Fill in the table below about Xavier

Loves	Likes a lot	Hates	Doesn't like

1. Faulty translation: spot and correct IN THE ENGLISH any translation mistakes you find below

a. J'adore les crevettes: *I hate prawns*

b. Je déteste le poulet: *I like meat*

c. J'aime le miel: *I don't like honey*

d. J'adore les oranges: *I love apples*

e. Les œufs sont dégoûtants: *Eggs are tasty*

f. Les bananes sont riches en vitamines: *Bananas are rich in protein*

g. Le poisson est très sain: *Fish is unhealthy*

h. Je préfère l'eau minérale: *I prefer tap water*

i. Je déteste les légumes: *I love vegetables*

j. J'adore le riz: *I love rice pudding*

k. Je n'aime pas les fruits: *I quite like fruit*

l. Les calamars frits sont délicieux: *Fried squid is salty*

2. Translate into English

a. Les crevettes sont délicieuses:

b. Le poisson est savoureux:

c. Le poulet est riche en protéines:

d. J'adore le riz:

e. La viande rouge est malsaine:

f. Des calamars frits:

g. Les œufs sont dégoûtants:

h. Je préfère l'eau gazeuse:

i. J'adore les crevettes:

j. Je n'aime pas les légumes:

k. J'aime les carottes:

l. Ce café est très sucré:

m. Une pomme dégoûtante:

n. Des oranges riches en vitamines:

3. Phrase-level translation En to Fr

a. Spicy chicken:

b. This coffee:

c. I quite like:

d. Very sweet:

e. A disgusting apple:

f. Some delicious oranges:

g. I don't like:

h. I love:

i. Tasty fish:

j. Mineral water:

k. Roast meat:

4. Sentence-level translation En to Fr

a. I like spicy chicken a lot.

b. I like oranges because they are healthy.

c. Meat is tasty but unhealthy.

d. This coffee is very sweet.

e. Eggs are disgusting.

f. I love oranges. They are delicious and rich in vitamins.

g. I love fish. It is tasty and rich in protein.

h. Vegetables are disgusting.

i. I prefer bananas.

j. This tea is sweet.

k. I love fizzy water.

Unit 11. Talking about food (Part 1): WRITING

1. Split sentences

J'aime le poulet 1	fruits
Je déteste les légumes car	**rôti 1**
Je préfère la	café est sucré
Ce	ils sont dégoûtants
J'aime assez les	délicieuses, mais malsaines
Les frites sont	les bananes
J'adore	viande

2. Rewrite the sentences in the correct order

a. le J' rôti poulet adore: *J'adore le poulet rôti*

b. les légumes déteste Je:

c. café Ce sucré est:

d. frites Les malsaines sont:

e. l' minérale préfère eau Je:

f. dégoûtants sont légumes Les:

g. beaucoup les aime oranges J' sont qu' parce délicieuses elles:

3. Spot and correct the grammar and spelling (there may be missing words)

a. J'aime les orange:

b. Je n'aime les légumes:

c. Les œufs dégoûtants:

d. J'adore ce café:

e. Je prefer les carottes:

f. Je déteste le viande:

4. Anagrams

a. goûtDéant

b. semugéL

c. deaVin: **viande**

d. ssonPio

e. anSi

f. ércSu

g. tiaL

5. Guided writing: write 3 short paragraphs describing the people's food taste below using the details in the box

Person	Loves	Quite likes	Doesn't like	Hates
Nathan	Chorizo because spicy	Milk because healthy	Red meat	Eggs because disgusting
Irène	Chicken because healthy	Oranges because sweet	Fish	Meat because unhealthy
Juliette	Honey because sweet	Fish because tasty	Fruit	Vegetables because boring

6. Write a paragraph on Raphaël in French using the third person singular

Name: Raphaël

Age: 18

Description: tall, good-looking, sporty, friendly

Occupation: student

Food he loves: chicken

Food he likes: vegetables

Food he doesn't like: red meat

Food he hates: fish

Grammar Time 8: MANGER/BOIRE
Talking about food Part 1

Boire *to drink*		
Je bois	**du café** *coffee*	
Tu bois	**du chocolat chaud** *hot chocolate*	
Il/elle/on boit	**du jus de fruits** *fruit juice*	
Nous buvons	**du jus d'orange** *orange juice*	
Vous buvez	**du jus de pomme** *apple juice*	**de temps en temps**
Ils/elles boivent	**du lait** *milk*	*from time to time*
	du thé *tea*	
	de l'eau *water*	
Manger *to eat*		**une fois par jour**
		once a day
	du chocolat *chocolate*	
	du fromage *cheese*	**une fois par semaine**
	des fruits *fruit*	*once a week*
	du miel *honey*	
	du pain *bread*	**tous les jours**
	du poisson *fish*	*every day*
Je mange	**du poulet rôti** *roast chicken*	
Tu manges	**du riz** *rice*	**tous les matins**
Il/elle/on mange	**de la salade verte** *green salad*	*every morning*
Nous mangeons	**de la viande** *meat*	
Vous mangez	**des chocolats** *chocolates*	**tous les soirs**
	des hamburgers *burgers*	*every evening*
Ils/elles mangent	**des légumes** *vegetables*	
	des œufs *eggs*	
	des bananes *bananas*	
	des crevettes *prawns*	
	des oranges *oranges*	
	des pommes *apples*	
	des tomates *tomatoes*	

1. Match

Je mange	They eat
Tu manges	She eats
Elle mange	We eat
Nous mangeons	You guys eat
Vous mangez	You eat
Ils mangent	I eat

2. Translate into English

a. Je mange des pâtes
b. Je mange souvent du riz
c. Je ne mange jamais de viande
d. Il mange beaucoup de poisson
e. Nous buvons de l'eau
f. Ils ne mangent jamais de poulet
g. Elle boit du jus de poire
h. Tu manges du poulet?
i. Que manges-tu?
j. Je bois souvent du jus de fruits

3. Spot and correct the mistakes

a. Mon père mangent des pâtes
b. Mon frère et moi ne mangez pas de fruits
c. Ma mère ne manges jamais de chocolat
d. Mes frères boit beaucoup de jus de fruits
e. Je ne boivent jamais de café
f. Ma sœur mangez de la viande tous les jours
g. Vous mangeons de la viande de cheval?
h. Que buvez-tu?

4. Complete

a. Mon père _____ beaucoup de fruits

b. Je ne _____ jamais de jus de kiwi

c. Tu _____ du poulet?

d. Ma mère et moi _____ beaucoup de pâtes

e. Mes parents _____ beaucoup d'eau

f. Ma sœur _____ beaucoup de chocolat chaud

g. Ma petite amie ne _____ jamais de vin

5. Translate into French

a. I eat pasta

b. We drink orange juice

c. What do you eat?

d. What do you guys drink?

e. We eat a lot of meat

f. They don't eat a lot of fish

g. She never eats vegetables

h. We drink lots of mineral water

6. Translate into French

a. I never eat red meat. I don't like it because it is unhealthy.

b. I rarely eat sausages. I don't like them because they are oily.

c. I drink fruit juice often. I love it because it is delicious and healthy.

d. I eat pizza every day. I love it because it is very tasty.

e. I rarely eat vegetables. They are healthy but I don't like them because they are disgusting.

f. I never drink tea or coffee because I don't like them.

 **THE LANGUAGE GYM**

UNIT 12 (Part 2)
Talking about food:
Likes/dislikes and why

Grammar Time: Agreement (food)

In this unit you will consolidate all that you learnt in the previous unit and learn how to say:
- What meals you eat every day and
- What you eat at each meal
- The full present indicative conjugation of 'prendre', 'déjeuner', 'dîner'
- 'This' and 'these' in French

You will revisit the following:
- The full present indicative conjugation of regular ER verbs + prendre
- Noun-to-adjective agreement

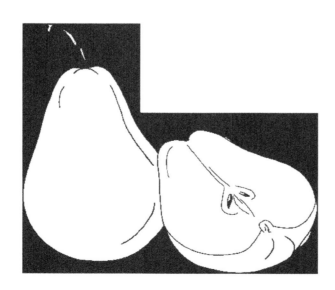

Unit 12
Talking about food: Likes/dislikes Part 2

Au petit-déjeuner, je prends *At breakfast I have* **Au déjeuner, je mange** *At lunch I eat* **Au goûter, je prends** *At tea time I have* **Au dîner, je mange** *At dinner I eat*	**du chocolat** *chocolate* **du café** *coffee* **du fromage** *cheese* **du jus de fruits** *fruit juice* **du lait** *milk* **du miel** *honey* **du poisson** *fish* **du poulet rôti** *roast chicken* **du riz** *rice* **du saumon** *salmon* **du thon** *tuna*	**car c'est** *because it is* **et je trouve cela** *and I find this*	**aigre** *acidic , sour* **amer** *bitter* **bon** *good* **dégoûtant** *disgusting* **délicieux** *delicious* **dur** *hard* **épicé** *spicy* **fade** *bland* **gras** *greasy* **juteux** *juicy* **léger** *light* **malsain** *unhealthy* **rafraîchissant** *refreshing* **riche en vitamines** *rich in vitamins* **sain** *healthy* **savoureux** *tasty* **sucré** *sweet*
Je bois *I drink* **Je mange** *I eat*	**de l'eau** *water* **de la pizza** *pizza* **de la salade verte** *green salad* **de la viande** *meat*		
Likes/dislikes **J'adore** *I love* **J'aime beaucoup** *I like a lot* **J'aime** *I like* **J'aime un peu** *I like a bit* **Je n'aime pas** *I don't like* **Je déteste** *I hate*	**les fruits** *fruit* **les hamburgers** *burgers* **les légumes** *vegetables* **les sandwichs au fromage** *cheese sandwiches* **les bananes** *bananas* **les crevettes** *prawns* **les oranges** *oranges* **les pêches** *peaches* **les pommes** *apples* **les saucisses** *sausages* **les tomates** *tomatoes*	**car ils/elles sont** *because they are*	**aigres** *acidic, sour* **amers/ères** *bitter* **bons/bonnes** *good* **dégoûtant(e)s** *disgusting* **délicieux/euses** *delicious* **dur(e)s** *hard* **salé(e)s** *salty* **sucré(e)s** *sweet*

Unit 12. Talking about food – Likes/Dislikes (Part 2): VOCABULARY

1. Match

L'eau	sandwich
Le poisson	water
Le riz	roast chicken
Le sandwich	fish
Le poulet rôti	cheese
La viande	honey
Les calamars	prawns
Les crevettes	strawberries
Le miel	sausages
Le fromage	rice
Les saucisses	fruit
Les fraises	squid
Les légumes	vegetables
Les fruits	meat

2. Complete with the missing words

a. J'aime les _____ *I like seafood*

b. J'adore la _____ *I love salad*

c. J'aime beaucoup les _____ *I like vegetables a lot*

d. J'aime les _____ *I like apples*

e. Ce _____ est délicieux *This chicken is delicious*

f. Cette _____ est très juteuse
This meat is very juicy

g. J'aime beaucoup les _____
I like bananas a lot

h. J'adore le _____ *I love honey*

i. Je n'aime pas le _____ *I don't like fish*

3. Complete with the missing letters

a. L'e _ _ : water

b. La v _ _ _ de: meat

c. Les fr _ _ _ _ : fruit

d. Le c _ _ _ _ n: lemon

e. La g _ _ _ e: ice cream

f. La po _ _ _ de terre: potato

g. Les fr _ _ _ _ de _ _ _ : seafood

h. La fr _ _ _ _ : strawberry

i. Fa _ _ mai _ _ _ : homemade

j. Le poi _ _ _ _ : fish

k. Jut _ _ _ : juicy

l. Le r _ _ : rice

m. La po _ _ e: apple

n. Le melo _ : melon

o. La cer _ _ _ : cherry

p. B _ _ : good

q. Le p _ _ _ : bread

r. É _ _ _ é: spicy

4. Match

Dur	Good
Frit	Delicious
Juteux	Juicy
Savoureux	Healthy
Sain	Hard
Bon	Disgusting
Délicieux	Fried
Gras	Sweet
Dégoûtant	Greasy
Sucré	Tasty
Amer	Bitter

5. Sort the items below into the appropriate category

a. délicieux	e. bon	i. pommes	m. amer	q. saumon	u. lait
b. sucré	f. crevettes	j. fraises	n. viande	r. poulet	v. pêches
c. riche	g. gras	k. dégoûtant	o. thon	s. salé	w. carottes
d. juteux	h. malsain	l. bananes	p. sain	t. épinards	x. fromage

Fruits	Légumes	Adjectifs	Poisson et viande	Produits laitiers

Unit 12. Talking about food – Likes/Dislikes (Part 2): READING

Je m'appelle Robert. Qu'est-ce que je mange? En général, je ne mange pas beaucoup au petit-déjeuner. Je prends seulement une pomme ou une banane et un peu de café. Je n'aime pas le café sucré.

À midi, en général, je prends un hamburger avec des frites et je bois de l'eau ou un jus de fruits. Les hamburgers ne sont pas sains, mais j'en raffole. J'adore le jus de fraise.

Après le collège, pour le goûter, je prends deux tartines avec de la confiture et du beurre et je bois une tasse de thé.

Pour le dîner, je mange beaucoup. D'habitude, je mange du riz avec des fruits de mer ou du poulet et des légumes et comme dessert un ou deux gâteaux. J'aimerais manger du fromage, car c'est délicieux, mais ma mère dit que ce n'est pas sain.

Je m'appelle Fernand. Qu'est-ce que je mange? En général, je ne mange pas beaucoup au petit-déjeuner. Seulement un œuf et une tasse de thé. J'aime le thé vert, avec beaucoup de sucre. Parfois, je bois un jus d'ananas.

À midi, je prends du poulet rôti avec des légumes et je bois de l'eau minérale. Je mange beaucoup de légumes car ils sont très sains et délicieux. J'aimerais manger des crevettes plus souvent, car je les adore!

Après le collège, pour le goûter je prends deux tartines avec du miel et je bois une tasse de thé. J'adore le miel, car c'est délicieux et riche en vitamines.

Pour le dîner, je mange beaucoup. D'habitude, je mange du riz avec des fruits de mer ou du poisson avec des légumes et comme dessert un ou deux gâteaux. Parfois je mange du poulet car c'est riche en protéines, mais je n'aime pas beaucoup ça, car ce n'est pas savoureux.

1. Find the French for the words below in Fernand's text.

a. Egg : o_____

b. Tea: t_____

c. Sweet: s_____

d. Sugar: s_____

e. Noon: m_____

f. Chicken: p_____

g. Roast: r_____

h. After: a_____

i. Cup: t_____

j. Honey: m_____

k. Vegetables: l_____

l. Healthy: s_____

m. Delicious: d_____

n. Dinner: d_____

o. Rice: r_____

p. Tasty: s_____

q. Cakes: g_____

2. Complete the following sentences based on Fernand's text

a. In general, at breakfast I only eat an _____ and drink a cup of _____

b. I like _____ tea with a lot of _____

c. At _____, for lunch I eat _____ _____ with _____ and drink _____ _____

d. I eat a lot of vegetables because they are _____ and delicious

e. As a snack I have two _____ with _____ and drink a _____ of tea

f. At dinner I usually eat _____, seafood or _____ with _____ and for dessert, one or two _____

3. Find the French for the following in Robert's text

a. I don't have much for breakfast

b. At noon I eat

c. Chicken

d. For dessert

e. One or two cakes

f. I would like to eat

g. A cup of tea

h. After school

i. Rice, seafood or fish

j. Toasts with jam/marmalade

k. Burgers are not healthy

l. Very sweet

m. An apple or a banana

4. Who says this, Robert or Fernand? Or both?

a. I would love to eat cheese – *Robert*

b. I love honey

c. I love strawberry juice

d. I don't eat much for breakfast

e. I would like to eat prawns

f. I have toasts with jam and butter

g. I am crazy about burgers

h. Burgers are not healthy

i. At dinner I eat a lot

j. I drink mineral water

k. His mother says cheese is not healthy

l. Sometimes I drink pineapple juice

Je m'appelle Eugène. Qu'est-ce que je mange? En général le matin je mange beaucoup: une banane, deux ou trois œufs, des tartines avec du jambon, un jus de fruits et une tasse de café. J'aime le café sucré.

À midi, en général, je prends seulement du riz avec du poulet ou des légumes et je bois de l'eau minérale ou un jus de fruits. J'adore le poulet, car c'est sain et riche en protéines. Parfois je mange des asperges. Je les aime car elles sont amères et riches en vitamines.

Après le collège pour le goûter, je prends deux tartines avec de la confiture de fraises et du beurre et je bois une tasse de thé.

Pour le dîner, je mange beaucoup. D'habitude des pâtes, de la viande avec des légumes et comme dessert une glace ou des gâteaux. J'aimerais manger du chocolat, car c'est délicieux, mais ma mère dit que ce n'est pas sain.

5. Answer the following questions on Eugène's text

a. How much does he eat at breakfast?

b. What does he eat? (4 things)

c. How does he like coffee?

d. What does he drink at lunch?

e. What does he have with rice?

f. Why does he like asparagus?

g. What does he put on toasts in the afternoon?

h. Why doesn't his mother allow him to eat chocolate?

---

6. Find in Eugène's text the following:

a. A word for dessert, starting with G:

b. A vegetable starting with A:

c. A drink starting with J:

d. A type of cold meat starting with J:

e. A fruit starting with B:

f. A dairy product starting with B:

g. An adjective starting with D:

h. A container starting with T:

i. A verb starting with M:

j. A fruit starting with F:

k. An adjective starting with S:

l. A meal starting with D:

Unit 12. Talking about food – Likes/Dislikes (Part 2): WRITING

1. Split sentences

Je mange toujours du poulet	avec du lait
Je mange des céréales	beurre
Je prends une tartine avec du	rôti
J'aime la salade	fruit préféré
La viande rouge est	délicieuse, mais malsaine
Le curry, c'est	ou du café
La banane est mon	verte
Je bois du thé	très épicé

2. Complete with the correct option

a. J'aime les _____, surtout le crabe.

b. En général, je _____ du riz avec du poulet.

c. Normalement _____ des céréales, dans la cuisine.

d. Je prends toujours du _____ rôti avec mon frère pour le déjeuner.

e. Pour le dîner, je mange du poisson et une salade _____.

f. Normalement, je prends un sandwich au _____.

g. J'aime beaucoup le _____ car c'est très sucré.

h. Le café est _____, mais j'adore ça.

i. Je n' _____ pas le lait, c'est dégoûtant!

verte	poulet	mange	amer	-
miel	fruits de mer	je prends	aime	fromage

3. Spot and correct the grammar and spelling mistakes note: in several cases a word is missing

a. En général, je un hamburger avec des frits.

b. Je bois de l'eau ou du jus fruits.

c. La viande rouge n'est pas saines, mais j'adore ça.

d. J'adore le jus d'oranges.

e. Après le collège, je prends deux tartine avec miel.

f. Je bois un tasse de thé avec du lait.

g. J'adore le miel car c'est délicieux et riche en vitamine.

h. Pour le dîner je manges du riz avec du poisson et des légumes.

i. J'aime les légumes car ils sont saines.

j. Mon poisson favori le saumon. C'est délicieuse!

4. Complete the words

a. Dé_____ *lunch*

b. D_____ *dinner*

c. P_____-d_____ *breakfast*

d. É_____ *spicy*

e. A_____ *bitter*

f. S_____ *sweet*

g. S_____ *healthy*

6. Sentence level translation EN - FR

a. I love fruit juice because it is sweet and refreshing.

b. I don't like salmon because it is disgusting.

c. At tea time I eat a cheese sandwich.

d. I always drink milk with honey. I like it because it's sweet.

e. I like fish, but chicken is not very tasty.

5. Guided writing: write 3 short paragraphs in the first person I using the details below

Person	Lunch	Location	With	After
Éloi	chicken and rice	the kitchen	brother	go to the beach
Cédric	burger	the dining room	sister	read a book
Juliette	salad	the garden	mother	listen to music

Grammar Time 9: ER Verbs (Part 2)
MANGER, DÉJEUNER, DÎNER + PRENDRE (RE verbs)

MANGER *to "eat"*	
Je mange *I "eat"* **Tu manges** *you* **Il/elle/on mange** *he/she/one* **Nous mangEons** *we* **Vous mangez** *you guys* **Ils/elles mangent** *they*	à l'extérieur *outside* à l'intérieur *inside* à la terrasse *at the terrace* chez moi *at home* en ville *in town*
DÉJEUNER *to have lunch*	
Je déjeune *I have lunch* **Tu déjeunes** *you* **Il/elle/on déjeune** *she/he/one* **Nous déjeunons** *we* **Vous déjeunez** *you guys* **Ils/elles déjeunent** *they*	à la cafétéria *at the lunch room* à la cantine *at the canteen* à la maison *at home* au réfectoire *at the refectory* au self *at the self-service restaurant*
DÎNER *to dine*	
Je dîne *I dine* **Tu dînes** **Il/elle/on dîne** **Nous dînons** **Vous dînez** **Ils/elles dînent**	chez moi *at home* chez un ami *at a friend's place* chez toi *at your place* au restaurant *at the restaurant*

PRENDRE – RE verb
(normally 'to take' but it translates as 'to have' in the context of food)

Je prends *I have* **Tu prends** **Il/elle/on prend** **Nous prenons** **Vous prenez** **Ils/elles prennent**	de la brioche *brioche* du café *coffee* un croissant *a croissant* le petit-déjeuner *breakfast* un pain au chocolat *a chocolate croissant*

1. Complete with the missing forms of 'manger'

a. Je ne _____ pas beaucoup. Je bois juste un café.

b. Ma mère _____ seulement un fruit.

c. Mes parents _____ seulement une tartine.

d. Ma sœur _____ des céréales avec du lait.

e. Mon frère et moi _____ deux tartines.

f. Que _____-tu?

g. Et vous, que _____-vous?

2. Spot and correct the errors with the verbs 'manger, 'déjeuner' and 'dîner'

a. Je ne manges pas d'épinards.

b. Ma mère dine souvent au restaurant.

c. Mon frère et moi ne dînent pas.

d. Mon père déjeunez à la maison.

e. Mon ami Paul ne manges jamais au petit-déjeuner.

f. Ma petite amie et moi mangez tous les jours à la cantine du collège.

g. Ma petite amie ne mangent jamais de viande pour le dîner.

3. Translate into English

a. Ma mère ne mange jamais de petit-déjeuner.

b. Ma sœur ne mange jamais de viande.

c. Parfois, je déjeune à la cantine.

d. En général, nous mangeons des œufs pour le dîner.

e. Que manges-tu normalement pour le déjeuner?

f. Je mange seulement une ou deux tartines le matin.

g. Pour le petit-déjeuner, mes frères mangent des céréales avec du lait.

5. Translate into French

a. For breakfast, I eat two eggs and one sausage. Also, I drink a coffee with milk.

b. My friend Paul doesn't eat much for lunch. Only chicken with rice.

c. For dinner, we eat a lot. We have a steak or fish with potatoes.

d. At noon, I drink a cup of coffee in the canteen with my girlfriend.

e. My girlfriend never eats red meat. She only eats fish or chicken.

f. My parents eat a lot for lunch. However, my brother and I only eat a salad.

g. My sisters don't eat much for dinner. Generally, they eat soup or vegetables.

4. Translate into French

a. *For dinner, I eat:* Pour le dîner, je _____.

b. *For lunch, we eat:* Pour le déjeuner nous _____.

c. *For breakfast she eats:* Pour le petit-déjeuner , elle _____.

d. *They dine:* Ils _____.

e. *She has lunch:* Elle _____.

f. *For dinner we eat:* Pour le dîner, nous _____.

g. *You have lunch in town:* Tu d_____ en ville.

h. *I dine at home:* Je d_____ à la maison.

Grammar Time 10: AGREEMENTS (Part 2)(Food)

Le *the* **Ce** *this*	café **MASC** chocolat fromage jus de fruits pain poisson porc *pork* poulet	**est** *is*	bon dégoûtant délicieux gras malsain épicé sain salé savoureux sucré
La *the* **Cette** *this*	confiture **FEM** pêche pomme salade viande		bonne dégoûtante délicieuse grasse malsaine épicée saine salée savoureuse sucrée
Les *the* **Ces** *these*	**MASC PLURAL** bonbons *sweets* fruits de mer *seafood* gâteaux légumes	**sont** *are*	bons dégoûtants délicieux gras malsains épicés sains salés savoureux sucrés
Les *the* **Ces** *these*	**FEM PLURAL** bananes boissons gazeuses *fizzy drinks* crevettes fraises *strawberries* oranges saucisses		bonnes dégoûtantes délicieuses grasses malsaines épicées saines salées savoureuses sucrées

1. Circle the correct option

	A	B
Le poisson est	sain	saine
Ce pain est	délicieux	délicieuse
Cette viande est	dur	dure
Le lait est	dégoûtant	dégoûtante
Le porc est	gras	grasse
Cette pomme est	bon	bonne
Cette fraise est	sucré	sucrée
Les fruits de mer sont	sains	saines

2. Write the opposite version of the adjectives below

Masculin	Féminin
	dégoûtante
délicieux	
	grasse
sucré	
épicé	
	saine
bons	
épicés	

3. Translate into English

a. Ces crevettes sont dégoûtantes.

b. Ces fraises sont délicieuses.

c. Ces fruits de mer sont très savoureux.

d. Cette pomme est dure.

e. Ce poisson est très bon.

f. Ce poulet est trop épicé.

4. Tick off the correct sentences and correct the incorrect ones

a. Ces crevettes sont très savoureuses.

b. L'agneau est très bon.

c. Ce poulet est trop salées.

d. Cette pomme est délicieuse.

e. Les fruits de mer sont très saines.

f. Ces saucisses sont très grasses.

5. Complete

a. Ce poisson est dégoût_____

b. Les pommes sont sain_____

c. La viande rouge est mals_____

d. Les gâteaux sont trop sucr_____

e. Ces fruits de mer sont très bon_____

f. Ces fraises sont délic_____

g. Ces bananes sont savour_____

h. Ces crevettes sont dégoût_____

6. Translate into French

a. This fish is disgusting.

b. These prawns are delicious.

c. This coffee is too sweet.

d. These sausages are very fatty.

e. These vegetables are very tasty.

f. Oranges are very healthy.

g. This chicken is very good.

Question Skills 2: Jobs/School bag/Food

1. Translate into English

a. Où manges-tu à midi?

b. Quel est le travail de ta mère?

c. Qu'est-ce que tu as dans ton sac?

d. Quelle est ta nourriture préférée?

e. Quelle est ta boisson préférée?

f. Tu manges beaucoup de viande?

g. Tu aimes le jus de pomme?

h. Pourquoi tu ne manges pas de légumes?

i. Tu manges souvent des desserts?

j. Quel est ton travail préféré?

k. Comment est ta sœur?

l. Avec qui manges-tu le petit-déjeuner en général?

2. Match the answers below to the questions in activity 1

a. Le jus de pomme.

b. Elle est intelligente et amusante.

c. J'aimerais être jardinier.

d. Oui, j'adore! C'est délicieux et sain.

e. Parce ce que je les déteste.

f. Le bœuf bourguignon.

g. Oui, tous les jours.

h. J'en mange deux fois par semaine.

i. Il y a deux livres, trois cahiers, une calculatrice et un agenda.

j. Ma mère est infirmière.

k. Dans la cantine du collège.

l. Avec mon meilleur ami.

3. Provide the questions to the following answers

a. Je ne mange pas de viande.

b. Je mange toujours des légumes car ils sont sains.

c. Je travaille comme pompier.

d. J'adore les fruits car ils sont délicieux et sains.

e. Je joue au foot au collège.

f. Je mange souvent des fruits de mer.

g. Je mange cinq fruits par jour.

h. Je suis de Martinique.

i. Je n'ai pas d'animaux.

j. Ma boisson préférée, c'est le jus de pomme.

k. Mon père travaille comme avocat.

l. Dans ma trousse, il y a seulement un stylo.

4. Complete

a. Qu'_____-ce q____ tu ____ d_____ t___ sac?　　e . Q_____ e_____ ta boisson préférée?

b. Qu'_____-ce q____ tu _____ comme travail?　　f. P_____ tu n'_____ pas la viande?

c. Tu _____ sou_____ des desserts?　　g. O__ m_____-tu à midi?

d. Qu'____-ce q___ tu _____ pour le dîner?　　h. Q_____ e_____ ta viande préférée?

UNIT 13
Talking about clothes and accessories I wear, how frequently and when

Grammar Time 11: -ER Verbs (Part 2) Porter + Agreements

Revision Quickie 3: Jobs, food, clothes and numbers 20-100

In this unit you will learn how to:

- Say what clothes you wear in various circumstances and places
- Describe various types of weather
- Give a wide range of words for clothing items and accessories
- Use a range of words for places in town
- Make the full present indicative conjugation of 'porter' (to wear)

You will revisit:
- Time markers
- Frequency markers
- Colours
- Self-introduction phrases
- Present indicative of 'Avoir'
- Noun-to-adjective agreement

UNIT 13
Talking about clothes

Quand il fait chaud *when it is hot* **Quand il fait froid** *when it is cold* **Quand je sors avec mon ami/amie** *when I go out with my friend* **Quand je sors avec mes amis** *when I go out with my friends* **Quand je joue au foot** *when I play football* **À la maison** *at home* **En discothèque** *at the nightclub* **Au collège** *at school* **Au gymnase** *at the gym* **A la plage** *at the beach* **Normalement** *normally* **En général** *in general* **Souvent** *often*	**je porte** *I wear* **il/elle porte** *he/she wears*	**une casquette** **FEM** *a baseball cap* **une chemise** *a shirt* **une ceinture** *a belt* **une cravate** *a tie* **une écharpe** *a scarf* **une jupe** *a skirt* **une montre** *a watch* **une robe** *a dress* **une veste** *a jacket* **une veste de sport** *a sports jacket*	**blanche** *white* **bleue** *blue* **grise** *grey* **jaune** *yellow* **marron** *brown* **noire** *black* **orange** *orange* **rouge** *red* **verte** *green*
		un chapeau *a hat* **MASC** **un collier** *a necklace* **un costume** *a suit* **un gilet** *a waistcoast* **un haut** *a top* **un jean** *jeans* **un maillot de bain** *a swimsuit* **un manteau** *a coat* **un pantalon** *trousers* **un pull** *jumper* **un short** *shorts* **un survêtement** *a tracksuit* **un tee-shirt** *a tee-shirt* **un tee-shirt sans manches** *tank top / vest* **un uniforme** *a uniform*	**blanc** *white* **bleu** *blue* **gris** *grey* **jaune** *yellow* **marron** *brown* **noir** *black* **orange** *orange* **rouge** *red* **vert** *green*
		PLURAL FEM **des bottes** *boots* **des boucles d'oreilles** *earrings* **des chaussettes** *socks* **des chaussures** *shoes* **des chaussures à talons hauts** *high heel shoes* **des chaussures de sport** *sports shoes* **des pantoufles** *slippers* **des sandales** *sandals*	**blanches** *white* **bleues** *blue* **grises** *grey* **jaunes** *yellow* **marron** *brown* **noires** *black* **orange** *orange* **rouges** *red* **vertes** *green*

Unit 13. Talking about clothes: VOCABULARY BUILDING

1. Match up

Des boucles d'oreilles	A baseball cap
Un tee-shirt	Trainers
Une robe	Trousers
Des chaussures de sport	A suit
Un pantalon	A T-shirt
Un costume	Earrings
Une casquette	A dress

2. Translate into English

a. Je porte un tee-shirt noir.

b. Je porte un costume gris.

c. Je ne porte pas de chaussures de sport.

d. Je porte une casquette bleue.

e. Je ne porte pas de montre.

f. Ma mère ne porte jamais de boucles d'oreilles.

g. Mon père porte un survêtement et des chaussures de sport.

h. Il ne porte jamais de costumes.

i. Je porte toujours des sandales.

j. Elle ne porte jamais de chapeaux.

3. Complete with the missing word

a. Chez moi, je _____ un _____
At home I wear a T-shirt

b. Au collège, je porte un _____ _____
At school I wear a black uniform

c. Au gymnase, je _____ un survêtement _____ *At the gym I wear a pink tracksuit*

d. À la plage, ___ porte un _____
At the beach I wear a swimsuit

e. _____ boîte, je porte une _____ noire et des _____ à _____ hauts blanches

In the club I wear a black dress and white high-heel shoes

f. Je _____ rarement des chaussures ___ _____
I rarely wear sports shoes

g. Je ne porte _____ de costumes
I never wear suits

4. Anagrams clothes and accessories

a. des setobt

b. une tremon

c. un mecostu

d. un peaucha.

e. des serussuach

f. une chmiese

g. naje

h. turecien

i. orths

k. bero

l. llup

m. maneaut

5. Associations – match each body part below with the words in the box, as shown in the examples

a. La tête *head* – **casquette**

b. Les pieds *feet* –

c. Les jambes *legs* –

d. Le cou *neck* –

e. Le torse *upper body* –

f. Les oreilles *ears* –

g. Le poignet *wrist* –

écharpe	cravate	chaussures	bottes
veste	chemise	chaussettes	**casquette**
boucles d'oreilles	pantalon	jupe	chapeau
gilet	montre	collier	tee-shirt

6. Complete

a. Je porte des bo_____
I wear boots

b. C_____ moi
At home

c. J'ai une _____
I have a watch

d. Je porte une c_____ rouge
I wear a red tie

e. Je porte un c_____ bleu
I wear a blue suit

f. Mon frère porte un g_____
My brother wears a waistcoat

g. Elle a une _____
She has a skirt

Unit 13. Talking about clothes: READING

Je m'appelle Charlotte. Je suis française. J'ai quinze ans. Je suis très sportive, donc j'ai beaucoup de vêtements de couleur et de styles différents. Je préfère les vêtements de bonne qualité, mais pas trop chers. En général, chez moi je porte un survêtement. J'en ai quatre ou cinq différents. Quand je sors avec mon petit ami, je porte des boucles d'oreilles, un collier, une robe rouge ou noire et des chaussures à talons hauts.

Je m'appelle Renaud. Je suis de La Rochelle. J'ai treize ans. J'adore acheter des vêtements, surtout des chaussures. J'ai beaucoup de chaussures de marque. J'adore les vêtements originaux. Quand il fait froid, en général, je porte un manteau et un pantalon. Parfois, je porte aussi une veste de sport. Quand il fait chaud, je porte des tee-shirts sans manches, un jean et des sandales ou des chaussures de sport.

Je m'appelle Léa. Je suis d'Auvergne. J'ai douze ans. J'achète toujours mes vêtements chez Zara. J'aime les jolis vêtements, mais pas trop chers. Je n'aime pas les vêtements de marque. Je porte toujours des vêtements de sport comme des survêtements, des tee-shirts sans manches et des chaussures de sport. Quand il fait froid, je porte une veste de sport et un pantalon. Quand il fait chaud, je porte une jupe et un haut de couleur.

Je m'appelle Michel. Je suis de Bourgogne. J'ai quatorze ans. Quand je vais au collège, je porte une chemise, un pantalon et des chaussures noires. Chez moi, en général, je porte un tee-shirt et un jean. J'ai beaucoup de tee-shirts et de jeans à la maison. Quand je vais au gymnase, je porte un tee-shirt sans manches, un short et des chaussures de sport. Quand je vais au centre commercial avec mes amis, je porte une veste, une chemise, un pantalon blanc ou gris, et des chaussures rouges ou blanches.

1. Find the French for the following in Charlotte's text

a. I am French

b. Sporty

c. Many clothes

d. Good quality clothes

e. A tracksuit

f. When I go out

g. With my boyfriend

h. Earrings

i. A red or black dress

j. High heel shoes

2. Find the French for the following in Michel's text

a. When I go

b. I wear a shirt

c. T-shirt and jeans

d. At home

e. Tank top

f. With my friends

g. A jacket

h. Grey trousers

i. Sports shoes

j. In general

3. Complete the following statements about Renaud

a. He is _____ years old

b. He loves buying _____

c. He has many branded _____

d. When it's cold he wears a _____ and some _____

e. Sometimes he also wears a _____ _____ _____

4. Answer in French the questions below about Léa

Quel âge a-t-elle?

Qu'est-ce qu'elle aime?

Où achète-t-elle ses vêtements?

Que porte-t-elle quand il fait froid?

Que porte-t-elle quand il fait chaud?

5. Find someone who

a. Who loves branded clothes?
b. Who is from Auvergne?
c. Who wears tank tops in the gym?
d. Who wears earrings when she goes out with her boyfriend?
e. Who has four or five different tracksuits?
f. Who has a lot of T-shirts and jeans at home?
g. Who is very sporty?
h. Who wears white or grey trousers at the shopping mall?

Unit 13. Talking about clothes: WRITING

1. Split sentences

Chez	tee-shirt et un short
Quand il fait	moi, je porte un survêtement
Au gymnase, je porte un	je porte des chaussures à talons hauts
Quand il fait chaud, je porte	froid, je porte une écharpe
Je ne porte jamais de jeans	un tee-shirt sans manches
Quand je vais en boîte,	Levi's
Je porte un pantalon	blanche
Je porte une chemise	noir

2. Complete with the correct option

a. _____ je sors avec mon _____ _____ , je porte de jolis vêtements confortables.

b. Au collège ____ _____ un uniforme bleu.

c. Au gymnase, je porte des _____ de sport.

d. À la plage, je porte un _____

e. Quand____ _____ chaud, je porte un _____ sans manches.

f. Chez moi, je porte ___ survêtement.

g. Quand il faid froid, je porte un _____.

h. Je ne porte _____ de bottes.

manteau	petit ami	un	je porte	quand
chaussures	jamais	il fait	maillot de bain	tee-shirt

3. Spot and correct the grammar and spelling mistakes note: in several cases a word is missing

a. Quand je sors mes parents, je porte une robe élégante.

b. Chez moi, je porte une survêtement.

c. J'ai beaucou chaussures.

d. Ma frère porte toujours des jean.

e. Au collège, un uniforme.

f. Je prefer les vêtements de marque.

g. Quand je vais centre commercial, en général, je porte une veste de sport.

h. Je porte toujours chaussures sport.

4. Complete the words

a. J_____ *skirt*

b. C_____ *suit*

c. M_____ *watch*

d. P_____ *trousers*

e. C_____ *shoes*

f. É_____ *scarf*

g. S_____ *tracksuit*

h. P_____ *slippers*

5. Guided writing: write 3 short paragraphs in the first person [I] using the details below

Person	Lives	Always wears	Never wears	Hates
Anne	Sarlat	black dresses	trousers	earrings
Georges	Quimper	white T-shirts	coats	watches
Jules	Douarnenez	jeans	shorts	scarves

6. Describe this person in French using the 3rd person

Name: Jean

Lives in: Toulouse

Age: 20

Pet: A black spider

Hair: blonde + green eyes

Always wears: suits

Never wears: jeans

At the gym wears: an Adidas tracksuit

Grammar Time 11: Key verbs (Part 2)
PORTER + AVOIR + AGREEMENTS

PORTER *to wear*	**FEM** **une casquette** *a baseball cap* **une chemise** *a shirt* **une ceinture** *a belt* **une cravate** *a tie* **une écharpe** *a scarf* **une jupe** *a skirt* **une montre** *a watch* **une robe** *a dress* **une veste** *a jacket* **une veste de sport** *a sports jacket*	**blanche** *white* **bleue** *blue* **grise** *grey* **jaune** *yellow* **marron** *brown* **noire** *black* **orange** *orange* **rouge** *red* **verte** *green*
je porte *I wear* **tu portes** *you wear* **il/elle/on porte** *he/she/one wears* **nous portons** *we wear* **vous portez** *you guys wear* **ils/elles portent** *they wear*		
AVOIR *to have* **j'ai** *I have* **tu as** *you have* **il/elle/on a** *he/she/one has* **nous avons** *we have* **vous avez** *you guys have* **ils/elles ont** *they have*	**MASC** **un chapeau** *a hat* **un collier** *a necklace* **un costume** *a suit* **un gilet** *a waistcoat* **un haut** *a top* **un jean** *jeans* **un maillot de bain** *a swimsuit* **un manteau** *a coat* **un pantalon** *trousers* **un pull** *jumper* **un short** *shorts* **un survêtement** *a tracksuit* **un tee-shirt** *a tee-shirt* **un tee-shirt sans manches** *tank top / vest* **un uniforme** *a uniform*	**blanc** *white* **bleu** *blue* **gris** *grey* **jaune** *yellow* **marron** *brown* **noir** *black* **orange** *orange* **rouge** *red* **vert** *green*

DRILLS

1. Complete with the missing verb endings

a. Je ne port__ jamais de jupes.

b. Que porte___-tu comme vêtements?

c. Mon frère port___ souvent un chapeau.

d. Mes parents o___ des vêtements de marque.

e. Mon prof port__ des vêtements moches.

f. Vous av____ beaucoup de jolis vêtements.

g. Au collège, nous port_____ un uniforme.

h. J'a__ beaucoup de jeans.

i. Que port____-vous en général?

j. Ma mère et moi av_____ beaucoup de vêtements.

k. Elle ne port___ jamais de robes élégantes.

l. Quand il fait froid, je port___ une écharpe.

 **THE LANGUAGE GYM**

2. Complete with the missing verbs

a. Ma mère _____ beaucoup de vêtements de marque. *My mother has a lot of branded clothes.*

b. Mes frères _____ aussi des tee-shirts. *My brothers also wear T-shirts.*

c. D'habitude, ma sœur _____ des jeans. *My sister usually wears jeans.*

d. Mes professeurs _____ toujours des costumes. *My teachers always wear suits.*

e. Ma petite amie _____ beaucoup de boucles d'oreilles. *My girlfriend has many earrings.*

f. Mon ami Paul et moi _____ beaucoup de tee-shirts noirs.
My friend Paul and I have many black T-shirts.

g. Mes parents _____ souvent des vêtements de sport. *My parents often wear sporty clothes.*

h. Mes cousins n'_____ pas beaucoup de vêtements. *My cousins don't have many clothes.*

---

3. Complete with the correct form of 'porter'

a. Je port__ une chemise.

b. Ma mère port__ une robe élégante.

c. Mes parents ne port____ pas de vestes de sport.

d. Mes frères port____ des jeans et des pulls.

e. Mon frère et moi port____ des shorts en été.

f. Ma sœur ne port____ jamais de jupes.

g. Que port____-tu à la plage?

h. Nous ne port_____ jamais de casquettes.

i. Au gymnase je port____ un survêtement.

---

4. Complete with the correct form of 'avoir'

a. Je n'____ pas beaucoup de vêtements.

b. Nous n'_____ pas de vêtements de marque.

c. Mon frère __ beaucoup de tee-shirts noirs.

d. Mon ami Paul n'__ pas assez de vêtements de sport.

e. Mes frères_____ beaucoup de cravates.

f. Ma mère____ beaucoup de robes élégantes.

g. J'___ un pull orange que j'adore.

h. Tu ___ une jolie jupe aujourd'hui.

---

5. Translate into English

a. Je ne porte jamais de tee-shirts.

b. Elle porte toujours des jeans.

c. Nous n'avons pas de robes élégantes.

d. Elles ont beaucoup de chaussures.

e. Il a beaucoup de chaussures de marque.

f. Ils portent toujours des chaussures de sport.

g. Que portes-tu au collège?

h. Au gymnase, elle porte un survêtement.

i. Vous avez des casquettes Adidas?

---

6. Translate into French

a. Do you have baseball caps?

b. We have many shoes.

c. I don't have an elegant dress.

d. My father has many suits and ties.

e. My mother never wears jeans.

f. I never wear trainers.

g. What clothes do you wear generally?

h. They never wear uniforms.

i. At the gym, I wear a tracksuit.

Revision Quickie 3: Jobs, food, clothes and numbers 20-100

1. Complete (numbers)

a. 100: ce

b. 90: qu

c. 30: tr

d. 50: ci

e. 80: qu

f. 60: so

g. 40: qu

2. Translate into English (food and clothes)

a. Le survêtement

b. Le jus de fruits

c. Le poulet

d. La jupe

e. Le porc

f. L'eau

g. La viande

h. Les fruits de mer

i. Le poisson

j. L'écharpe

k. Les chaussures

l. Les légumes

m. Le jus de tomate

n. Le déjeuner

3. Write in a word for each letter in the categories below as shown in the example *(there is no obvious word for the greyed out boxes!)*

LETTRE	Vêtements	Nourriture et boissons	Numéros	Travail
C				
T				
V				
M				
A				

4. Match

je porte	my name is
j'ai	I drink
je suis	breakfast
goûter	I live
je mange	I work
je bois	I have
petit-déjeuner	I dine
je travaille	there is
je dîne	I am
je vis	afternoon snack
il y a	I wear
je m'appelle	I eat

5. Translate into English

a. Je ne porte jamais de jupes.

b. Au goûter, je mange une tartine avec du miel.

c. Je travaille comme avocat.

d. Je bois souvent du café.

e. Je ne bois pas de boissons gazeuses.

f. Je mange toujours des œufs au petit-déjeuner.

g. Ma mère est femme d'affaires.

h. Je n'ai pas beaucoup de vêtements de marque.

i. Je ne mange pas beaucoup au dîner, seulement une salade.

UNIT 14
Saying what I and others do in our free time

Grammar Time: Jouer, Faire and Aller

In this unit you will learn how to say:

- What activities you do using the verbs 'jouer' (play), 'faire' (do) and 'aller' (go)
- Other free time activities

You will revisit:
- Time and frequency markers
- Weather
- Expressing likes/dislikes
- Adjectives
- Pets

UNIT 14
Saying what I (and others) do in our free time

Je joue *I play*	**au basket** *basketball* **au foot** *football* **au tennis** *tennis* **aux cartes** *cards* **aux échecs** *chess* **avec des amis** *with some friends*	**de temps en temps** *from time to time* **deux fois par semaine** *twice a week*
Je fais *I do*	**du footing** *jogging* **du ski** *skiing* **du sport** *sport* **du vélo** *cycling* **de l'équitation** *horse riding* **de l'escalade** *rock climbing* **de la natation** *swimming* **de la randonnée** *hiking*	**pendant le week-end** *during the weekend* **tous les jours** *every day* **tous les samedis** *every Saturday*
Je vais *I go*	**au centre commercial** *to the mall* **au centre sportif** *to the sports centre* **au gymnase** *to the gym* **au parc** *to the park* **à la campagne** *to the countryside* **à la montagne** *to the mountain* **à la pêche** *fishing* **à la piscine** *to the pool* **à la plage** *to the beach* **chez des amis** *to my friends' house -plural* **en boîte** *clubbing*	**tous les soirs** *every evening* **tous les week-ends** *every weekend* **une fois par mois** *once a month*

Unit 14. Free time: VOCABULARY BUILDING – Part 1 Weather

1. Match up

Je joue aux échecs	I go horse riding
Je fais du footing	I play chess
Je fais de l'équitation	I play basketball
Je joue aux cartes	I go hiking
Je fais du vélo	I go swimming
Je fais de la natation	I go biking
Je fais de la randonnée	I go jogging
Je joue au basket	I play cards

2. Complete with the missing word

a. Je joue aux _____ *I play chess*

b. _____ de l'équitation *I go horse riding*

c. _____ aux cartes *I play cards*

d. Je fais du _____ *I cycle*

e. Je joue au _____ *I play basketball*

f. Je vais à la _____ *I go fishing*

g. Je fais de la _____ *I go hiking*

h. Je fais de l'_____ *I go rock climbing*

i. Je fais du _____ *I go jogging*

j. Je ne fais pas mes _____ *I don't do my homework*

je joue	basket	pêche	escalade	je fais
devoirs	vélo	échecs	randonnée	footing

3. Translate into English

a. Je fais du vélo tous les jours.

b. Je fais souvent de la randonnée.

c. Je fais de l'escalade deux fois par mois.

d. Je ne fais jamais d'équitation.

e. Quand il fait mauvais, je joue aux cartes ou aux échecs.

f. Je joue souvent au basket.

g. Je fais rarement du footing.

h. Je vais souvent chez mon ami.

i. Je vais à la plage tous les jours.

j. Je vais à la pêche une fois par semaine.

4. Broken words

a. Je fais de l éq_____ *I go horse riding*

b. Je fais de la na_____ *I go swimming*

c. Je vais à la pê_____ *I go fishing*

d. Je fais du vé_____ *I cycle*

e. Je joue aux éc_____ *I play chess*

f. Je vais en bo_____ *I go clubbing*

g. Je joue aux ca_____ *I play cards*

h. Je fais de l'esc_____ *I do rock climbing*

5. 'Je fais', 'Je joue'

a. _____ au basket

b. _____ du vélo

c. _____ aux échecs

d. _____ aux cartes

e. _____ de la natation

f. _____ du footing

g. _____ au tennis

h. _____ de l'escalade

6. Bad translation: spot any translation errors and fix them

a. Je ne vais jamais en boîte: *I often go clubbing*

b. Je joue souvent aux cartes: *I often play chess*

c. Je fais rarement de l'escalade: *I go swimming rarely*

d. Quand il fait beau, je fais du footing:
When the weather is nice, I go hiking

e. Je fais du vélo une fois par semaine: *I go biking every day*

f. Je ne joue jamais aux échecs: *I often play chess*

g. Je fais de la randonnée une fois par mois: *I never go hiking*

h. Je fais souvent de la natation: *I go swimming from time to time*

 THE LANGUAGE GYM

Unit 14. Free time: READING

Je m'appelle Thomas. Je suis allemand. Pendant mon temps libre, je fais beaucoup de sport. Mon sport préféré, c'est l'escalade. J'en fais tous les jours. Quand il fait mauvais, je reste chez moi *[I stay at home]* et je joue aux échecs ou aux cartes. J'aime aussi beaucoup jouer aux jeux vidéo ou à la Playstation. Je joue souvent sur ma Playstation.

Je m'appelle Verónica. Je suis espagnole, de Barbastro. Je suis rousse et très sympathique et amusante, mais je ne suis pas très sportive. Je préfère lire des livres *[read books]*, jouer aux jeux vidéo ou aux échecs et écouter de la musique. Par contre, quand il fait beau, parfois je fais du footing au parc de mon quartier ou je joue au tennis avec mon frère. Je n'aime pas aller au gymnase, ni à la piscine. Je déteste la natation car je n'aime pas l'eau.

Je m'appelle Jennifer. Je suis anglaise. Pendant mon temps libre, j'aime beaucoup lire des livres et des journaux. J'aime aussi jouer aux cartes et aux échecs. Je ne suis pas très sportive, mais parfois je vais au gymnase. De plus, quand il fait beau le week-end je fais de la randonnée à la campagne avec mon chien. Mon chien s'appelle Doug et il est grand et blanc. Il est très amusant!

Je m'appelle Ronan. Je suis français. J'adore faire du vélo. Je fais du vélo avec mes amis tous les jours. C'est mon sport favori. Parfois, je fais de l'escalade, du footing ou de la randonnée. Je n'aime pas le tennis, ni le football. Je déteste aussi la natation. Je fais de la natation très rarement. Deux fois par semaine, je vais en boîte avec mon ami Julien. J'adore danser!

1. Find the French for the following in Thomas' text

a. I do a lot of sport

b. My favourite sport

c. Rock climbing

d. Every day

e. When the weather's bad

f. I play chess

g. Also

h. I play on my Playstation

2. Find the French in Ronan's text for

a. I love biking

b. with my friends

c. sometimes

d. I do swimming

e. I go clubbing

f. I go rock climbing

g. with my friend Julien

3. Complete the following statements about Verónica

a. She is from _____

b. She is not very _____

c. She plays videogames or _____

d. When the weather is nice she goes _____

e. She also plays tennis with her _____

4. List 7 details about Jennifer

1
2
3
4
5
6
7

5. Find someone who...

a. ...enjoys reading newspapers

b. ...hates swimming

c. ...does a lot of sport

d. ...goes to the gym

e. ...goes clubbing twice a week

 **THE LANGUAGE GYM**

Unit 14. Free time: TRANSLATION

1. Gapped translation

a. **Je ne vais jamais en boîte**: *I _____ go clubbing*

b. **Je joue souvent au basket**: *I often play _____*

c. **Je ne joue jamais au tennis**: *I _____ play tennis*

d. **Je joue aux _____**: *I play chess*

e. **Je joue aux _____**: *I play cards*

f. **Parfois, je fais du vélo**: *_____, I go cycling*

g. **Je ne fais jamais d'escalade**:
I never do _____

h. **Quand il fait _____, je fais du footing**:
When the weather is nice, I go jogging

2. Translate to English

a. Jamais

b. Parfois

c. Quand il fait mauvais

d. Chez mon ami

e. Rarement

f. Tous les jours

g. Je fais de la randonnée

h. Je vais en boîte

i. Je vais à la pêche

3. Translate into English

a. Je ne vais jamais à la pêche avec mon père.

b. Je joue aux cartes avec mon frère.

c. Je fais de la randonnée avec ma mère.

d. Je joue aux échecs avec mon meilleur ami.

e. Je ne joue jamais à la Playstation avec mes amis.

f. Je vais en boîte tous les samedis.

4. Translate into French

a. Bike: V

b. Rock climbing: E

c. Basketball: B

d. Fishing: P

e. Homework: D

f. Videogames: J

g. Chess: E

h. Cards: C

i. Hiking: R

j. Jogging: F

5. Translate into French

a. I 'do' jogging.

b. I play chess.

c. I 'do' rock climbing.

d. I 'do' swimming.

e. I 'do' horse riding.

f. I do my homework.

g. I go clubbing.

h. I play videogames.

i. I 'do' cycling.

j. I 'do' hiking.

Unit 14. Free time: WRITING

1. Split sentences

Je ne fais	parc
Je joue souvent	de sport
Je vais chez	jamais d'escalade
Je fais du footing au	aux échecs
Je joue aux	vélo
Je fais beaucoup	mon ami Paul
Je fais du	chez moi
Je fais mes devoirs	cartes

2. Complete the sentences

a. Je ne _____ jamais de footing.

b. Parfois, je _____ aux échecs.

c. Je _____ de l'escalade de temps en temps.

d. Je _____ souvent de l'équitation.

e. Je joue au tennis _____ _____ jours.

f. Je vais _____ mon ami.

g. Pendant mon _____ libre.

h. Je _____ mes devoirs à la maison.

i. Je _____ à la campagne avec ma famille.

3. Spot and correct mistakes note: in some cases a word is missing

a. Je joue au tenis.

b. Je joue au échec.

c. Je vais chez ami.

d. Je fais jamais du vélo.

e. Je vais mes devoirs.

f. Je fais à la campagne.

g. Je vais des randonnées.

4. Complete the words

a. Éc_____

b. Bas_____

c. Ran_____

d. Jeux-_____

e. Équi_____

f. Jam_____

g. Sou_____

h. Rar_____

5. Write a paragraph for each of the people below in the first person singular (I):

Name	Sport I do	When	Who with	Where	Why I like it
Jeanne	Hiking	Every day	With my boyfriend	In the countryside	It's fun
Dylan	Tennis	Often	With my friend James	At home	It's healthy
Alexandre	Jogging	When the weather is nice	Alone	In the park	It's relaxing

Grammar Time 12: Jouer, Faire and Aller (Part 1)

Jouer *to play*		
je joue *I play*	**au basket** *basketball*	
tu joues *you play*	**au foot** *football*	
il/elle joue *he/she plays*	**au tennis** *tennis*	
nous jouons *we play*	**aux cartes** *cards*	**de temps en temps** *from time to time*
vous jouez *you guys play*	**aux échecs** *chess*	
ils/elles jouent *they play*	**avec des amis** *with some friends*	
Faire *to do*		**deux fois par semaine** *twice a week*
je fais *I do*	**du footing** *jogging*	
tu fais	**du ski** *skiing*	**pendant le week-end** *during the week-end*
il/elle fait	**du sport** *sport*	
nous faisons	**du vélo** *cycling*	**tous les jours** *every day*
vous faites	**de l'équitation** *horse riding*	
ils/elles font	**de l'escalade** *rock climbing*	**tous les samedis** *every Saturday*
	de la natation *swimming*	
	de la randonnée *hiking*	
Aller *to go*		**tous les soirs** *every evening*
	au centre commercial *to the mall*	
	au centre sportif *to the sports centre*	**tous les week-ends** *every week-end*
je vais *I go*	**au gymnase** *to the gym*	
tu vas	**au parc** *to the park*	
il/elle va	**à la campagne** *to the countryside*	**une fois par mois** *once a month*
nous allons	**à la montagne** *to the mountain*	
vous allez	**à la pêche** *fishing*	
ils/elles vont	**à la piscine** *to the pool*	
	à la plage *to the beach*	
	chez des amis *to my friends' house -plural*	
	en boîte *clubbing*	

1. Match

Je fais	She does
Tu fais	We do
Il fait	You do
Elle fait	He does
Nous faisons	I do
Vous faites	They do
Ils font	You guys do

3. Write the correct form of JOUER (To play)

a. I play: _____

b. You play: _____

c. She plays: _____

d. We play: _____

e. You guys play: _____

f. They (fem) play: _____

g. My brothers play: _____

h. You and I play _____

i. He and I play: _____

5. Spot and correct the translation errors

a. Je vais à la pêche: *You go fishing*

b. Tu vas à l'église: *He goes to church*

c. Nous allons au centre commercial:
You guys go to the shopping mall

d. Je ne vais jamais chez Marine:
We never go to Marine's house

e. Ils vont au cinéma une fois par semaine:
She goes to the cinema once a week

2. Complete with the correct ending

a. Je ne fai___ jamais mes devoirs.

b. Mon père jou___ souvent au foot.

c. Quel sport fai___-tu?

d. Nous ne jou____ jamais au tennis.

e. Que fai____-vous aujourd'hui?

f. Mes frères jou____ souvent à la Playstation.

g. Je ne jou___ jamais aux jeux vidéo.

h. Mon frère aîné fai___ des arts martiaux.

i. Mes sœurs ne jou___ pas aux échecs.

j. Ma mère et moi jou____ aux cartes ensemble.

k. Je fai___ du vélo tous les jours.

4. Complete with the first person of FAIRE, ALLER or JOUER: *je fais, je vais, je joue*

a. Je ne _____ jamais au basket.

b. Je _____ du sport tous les jours.

c. Je _____ au volley une fois par semaine.

d. Je _____ rarement aux cartes.

e. Je ne _____ jamais de vélo.

f. Je _____ à la Playstation de temps en temps.

g. Je _____ très rarement à la pêche.

h. Je _____ souvent de l'escalade.

i. Je _____ au stade avec mon père.

6. Complete the forms of ALLER below

a. Je_____ à la pêche — *I go fishing*

b. Ils _____ à l'église — *They go to church*

c. Nous _____ à la plage — *We go to the beach*

d. Ils _____ à la piscine — *They go to the pool*

e. Où _____-tu? — *Where are you going?*

7. Complete with *fait, joue* or *va* as appropriate

a. Ma mère ne _____ jamais de sport.

b. Mon père _____ rarement à l'église.

c. Mon frère _____ à la mosquée tous les vendredis.

d. Ma grand-mère ne _____ jamais aux cartes avec moi.

e. Mon frère aîné _____ des arts martiaux.

f. Mon ami Paul _____ souvent à la Playstation.

g. Mon petit frère _____ souvent du vélo.

h. Mon grand-père _____ à la plage tous les jours.

9. Translate into English

a. Je ne joue jamais au foot.

b. Elle fait toujours ses devoirs.

c. Nous allons à l'église tous les dimanches.

d. Ils ne vont pas souvent à la piscine.

e. Quand il fait beau, ils vont au parc.

f. Il ne joue jamais aux échecs.

g. Quand il fait mauvais, je vais au gymnase.

8. Complete with *font, jouent* or *vont* as appropriate

a. Mes parents ne _____ jamais au basket.

b. Mes frères ne _____ pas de sport.

c. Mes sœurs ne _____ jamais au foot.

d. Ma mère et mon père _____ souvent aux cartes.

e. Mes cousins _____ des arts martiaux tous les week-ends.

f. Elles _____ souvent à la pêche.

g. Mes oncles _____ à l'église très rarement.

h. Mes amis ne_____ jamais de l'escalade avec moi.

i. Ils _____ du vélo?

j. Mes amies, Léa et Laura _____ aux échecs.

k. Elles _____ souvent à la piscine.

10. Translate into French

a. We never go to the swimming pool.

b. They do sport rarely.

c. She plays basketball every day.

d. When the weather is nice, I do jogging.

e. I rarely do cycling.

f. I often do rock climbing.

g. My father and I often play badminton.

h. My sister plays tennis twice a week.

i. I go to the swimming pool on Saturdays.

j. When the weather is bad, I go to the gym.

k. They rarely do their homework.

l. We never play chess.

UNIT 15
Talking about weather and free time

GRAMMAR TIME: Jouer / Faire / Aller
Question skills: Clothes / Free time / Weather

In this unit you will learn how to say:
- What free-time activities you do in different types of Weather
- Where you do them **and** who with
- Words for places in town

You will also learn how to ask and answer questions about:
- Clothes
- Free time
- Weather

You will revisit:
- Sports and hobbies
- The verbs 'faire', 'aller' and 'jouer' in the present indicative
- Pets
- Places in town
- Clothes
- Family members
- Numbers from 1 to 100

Unit 15
Talking about weather and free time

Quand j'ai le temps *When I have time* **Quand le ciel est dégagé** *When the sky is clear* **Quand il y a des nuages** *When it is cloudy* **Quand il fait beau** *When the weather is good* **Quand il fait mauvais** *When the weather is bad* **Quand il fait chaud** *When it is hot* **Quand il fait froid** *When it is cold* **Quand il y a du soleil** *When it is sunny* **Quand il y a du vent** *When it is windy* **Quand il y a du brouillard** *When it is foggy* **Quand il y a de l'orage** *When it is stormy* **Quand il pleut** *When it rains* **Quand il neige** *When it snows* **Parfois** *Sometimes* **Pendant la semaine** *During the week* **Le week-end** *At the weekend*	**je joue** *I play* **mon amie Marie joue** *my friend Marie plays*	**au basket** *basketball* **au foot** *football* **au tennis** *tennis* **aux cartes** *cards* **aux échecs** *chess* **avec mes amis** *with my friends* **avec ses amis** *with her friends*
	je fais *I do* **mon ami Lionel fait** *my friend Lionel does*	**du footing** *jogging* **du ski** *skiing* **du sport** *sport* **du vélo** *cycling* **de l'équitation** *horse riding* **de l'escalade** *rock climbing* **de la natation** *swimming* **de la randonnée** *hiking* **mes/ses devoirs** *my/his homework*
	je vais *I go* **mon amie Anna va** *my friend Anna goes*	**au centre commercial** *to the mall* **au centre sportif** *to the sports centre* **au gymnase** *to the gym* **au parc** *to the park* **à la campagne** *to the countryside* **à la montagne** *to the mountain* **à la pêche** *fishing* **à la piscine** *to the pool* **à la plage** *to the beach* **chez mon ami** *to my friend's house* **chez son ami** *to her friend's house* **en boîte** *clubbing*
	je reste *I stay* **mon ami Philippe reste** *my friend Philippe stays*	**chez moi** *at my home* **dans ma chambre** *in my room* **chez lui** *at his home* **dans sa chambre** *in his room*

Unit 15. Talking about weather and free time VOCABULARY BUILDING 1

1. Match up

Quand	It's cold
Il fait froid	It's hot
Il fait chaud	The sky is clear
Il fait beau	When
Il fait mauvais	It's good weather
Le ciel est dégagé	It's raining
Il pleut	It's bad weather

2. Translate into English

a. Quand il fait froid:

b. Quand il pleut:

c. Le ciel est dégagé:

d. Quand il fait chaud:

e. Quand il neige:

f. Quand il fait beau:

g. Quand il y a du brouillard:

h. Je joue au tennis:

i. Je fais du ski:

j. Quand il fait mauvais:

3. Complete with the missing word

a. Quand il fait_____ *When it's bad weather*

b. Quand il _____ et il fait _____
When it rains and is cold

c. Quand _____ du soleil et il fait _____
When it is sunny and hot

d. Quand il y a de l'orage, je _____ chez moi
When it is stormy, I stay at home

e. Quand il fait_____, je vais au parc
When it's good weather, I go to the park

f. Quand il _____, je fais du ski à la montagne
When it snows, I ski on the mountain

g. Quand il fait _____, mon ami reste chez lui
When the weather is bad, my friend stays at home

h. J'aime quand il y a du _____
I like it when it's sunny

4. Anagrams weather

a. fiord   g. leiosl

b. auchd   h. tenv

c. nieeg   i. llardbroui

d. eiulp   j. gesaun

e. déégga   k. rageo

f. vaismau   l. uaeb

5. Associations – match each weather word below with the clothes/activities in the box

a. Mauvais temps: orage, vent, pluie –

b. Beau temps: soleil et chaud –

c. Neige et froid –

bottes de neige	je reste chez moi	je fais du ski	la plage
je ne fais rien	je porte un short	je regarde la télé	je porte un chapeau
la montagne	écharpe	pyjama	maillot de bain

6. Complete

a. Il fait _____ *It's good weather*

b. Je reste _____ moi *I stay at home*

c. Quand il _____ *When it rains*

d. J' _____ quand il y a du soleil *I like it when it's sunny*

e. Je _____ à la plage *I go to the beach*

f. Quand il y a de l'_____
When it's stormy

g. Quand le _____ est dégagé
When the sky is clear

h. Quand il y a des _____
When it is cloudy

Unit 15. Talking about weather and free time: VOCABULARY BUILDING 2

1. Match up

Je joue au tennis	I go to the park
Je joue aux cartes	In his/her bedroom
Je fais du footing	He goes fishing
Je vais au parc	I play tennis
Il va à la pêche	I do jogging
Dans sa chambre	I play cards
Je reste chez moi	Swimming
La natation	I stay at home

2. Complete with the missing word

a. Je reste dans _____ chambre *I stay in my bedroom*

b. Mon ami _____ à la plage *My friend goes to the beach*

c. Je vais _____ mon _____ *I go to my friend's house*

d. Parfois, je vais au _____ _____
Sometimes, I go to the sports centre

e. Pendant la _____, je fais toujours mes devoirs
During the week, I always do my homework

f. J'aime les _____ car je joue avec mes amis
I like weekends because I play with my friends

g. Mon amie Léa _____ toujours chez son _____
My friend Léa always goes to her friend's house

h. Je fais toujours de la _____
I always do hiking

3. Translate into English

a. La maison de mon ami.

b. Je fais de l'équitation.

c. Le ciel est dégagé.

d. Je fais de l'escalade.

e. Elle fait du footing.

f. Il va au centre sportif.

g. Je vais à la piscine.

h. Je fais du sport.

4. Anagrams activities

a. foinotg   g. tecars

b. natiaton   h. chécse

c. onnéerand   i. cernte corcmeialm

d. équtiatino   j. îotbe

e. sketab   k. cheêp

f. toof   l. trops

5. Broken words

a. Je _____ a__ f_____ a_____ mes a_____
I play football with my friends

b. M__ t_____ M_____ j_____ aux c_____
My aunt Marie plays cards

c. Je v_____ c_____ m___ a_____
I go to my friend's house

d. J_____ v__ a__ c_____ s_____
Jean goes to the sports centre

e. Je _____ de l'é_____ a_____ m___
c_____   *I do horse riding with my horse*

f. M___ a_____ r_____ c_____ m_____
My friend stays at my place

6. Complete

a. Je fais mes _____
I do my homework

b. Il _____ à la maison
He stays at home

c. Il fait de la _____
He does swimming

d. Je vais ___ gymnase
I go to the gym

e. __ _____ à la piscine
I go to the pool

f. Je reste à la _____
I stay at home

Unit 15. Talking about weather and free time: READING

Je m'appelle Pierre. Je suis de France. J'ai onze ans. Je suis très sportif, donc j'aime quand il fait beau. Quand il y a du soleil, je vais souvent au parc avec mes amis et nous jouons au foot. Quand il fait chaud, je vais à la plage avec mon chien. Il est petit, noir et amusant. Quand je vais à la plage, je porte un maillot de bain, des sandales et un chapeau.

Je m'appelle Isabelle. Je suis de Rome, en Italie. J'ai quinze ans. J'adore acheter des vêtements. J'adore quand il y a de l'orage, car je reste à la maison avec mon frère aîné et nous jouons aux jeux vidéo ou aux cartes. Je n'aime pas quand il fait froid, car je n'aime pas porter un manteau et une écharpe. Chez moi, j'ai un chien, un chat et un perroquet qui parle italien!

Je m'appelle Anna. Je suis du Brésil. J'ai douze ans. J'adore chanter pendant mon temps libre. Quand il fait froid, je vais au centre commercial avec mes amies. Je porte un manteau, une écharpe et des bottes. J'adore le froid! Mon film préféré est Frozen 2. Quand il fait chaud, je reste chez moi. Je ne vais jamais à la plage car je déteste ça!

Je m'appelle Chloé. Je suis française. J'ai quatorze ans. Quand il fait chaud et que le ciel est dégagé, je vais à la piscine et je fais de la natation. Parfois, je vais à la pêche avec mon père sur son bateau. C'est un peu ennuyeux, mais j'aime ça. Le soir, je vais en boîte avec mes amis. Quand je vais en boîte, en général je porte un haut et un jean. Mon amie s'appelle Sophie. Elle est sympathique et intelligente. S'il fait mauvais, elle reste toujours chez elle et fait ses devoirs.

1. Find the French for the following in Pierre's text

a. I am from

b. I am 11

c. I like

d. when

e. it is sunny

f. I often go to the park

g. with my dog

h. small and black

i. a swimsuit

j. the beach

2. Find the French for the following in Chloé's text

a. when it's hot

b. the sky is clear

c. I swim

d. I go fishing

e. a bit boring

f. I go clubbing

g. a top

h. is called

i. stays

j. in her house

3. Complete the following statements about Isabelle's text

a. She is _____ years old.

b. She loves buying _____.

c. She loves it when there are _____.

d. When it's stormy she plays _____ or _____ with her _____ brother.

e. Isabelle does not like _____weather.

f. Her pet can _____ Italian.

4. Answer in French the questions below about Anna

a. D'où est-elle?

b. Quel âge a-t-elle?

c. Que fait-elle pendant son temps libre?

d. Quel type de temps aime-t-elle?

e. Que fait-elle quand il fait froid?

f. Que fait-elle quand il fait chaud?

g. Quel est son film préféré?

5. Find someone who

a. Likes to go fishing?

b. Who is from France? (2)

c. Who loves really cold weather?

d. Who has three pets at home?

e. Who loves storms?

f. Who wears jeans to go out?

g. Who goes to the beach with an animal?

h. Who never goes to the beach?

i. Who owns a boat?

Unit 15. Talking about weather and free time: WRITING

1. Split sentences

J'aime quand	soleil, je vais à la plage
Je n'aime pas	un manteau et une écharpe
Quand il fait beau,	il fait froid
Quand il fait très froid, je porte	la pluie
J'adore l'	je fais du ski
Quand il fait mauvais,	je reste chez moi
Quand il y a du	orage
Quand il neige,	je vais au parc

2. Complete with the correct option

a. _____ il fait froid, je porte une écharpe. Je _____ ça!

b. Pendant la _____, je fais mes devoirs.

c. Quand _____ mauvais, je _____ à la maison.

d. Quand il _____, je vais à la _____ pour faire du ski.

e. Quand il fait _____, je vais à la plage.

f. Quand _____ est dégagé, je fais de la randonnée à la campagne.

g. Quand il fait mauvais, mon ami Julien reste _____ lui.

chaud	neige	reste	montagne	semaine
déteste	il fait	quand	le ciel	chez

3. Spot and correct the grammar and spelling mistakes note: in several cases a word is missing

a. Quand il y a du vent, je vais gymnase avec ma ami.

b. Quand il y a des nuages, mon ami Jean fais du vélo.

c. J'adore les orages car ils sont divertissant.

d. Quand il fait mauvais, mon ami reste lui.

e. Quand il neige, je ne joue au basket.

f. Le week-end, je vais plage avec mon chien.

g. Quand il fait beau, je vais à la campagne et je porte un tee-shirt blanche.

h. Je portes toujours des chaussures de sport quand je joues au foot.

4. Complete the words

a. F_____ *cold*

b. C_____ *hot*

c. N_____ *clouds*

d. Q_____ *when*

e. O_____ *storms*

f. V_____ *wind*

5. Guided writing: write 3 short paragraphs in the first person I using the details below

Person	Lives	Weather	Activity	With
Éloi	Grenoble	good weather	go to the park	friends
Sandrine	Le Mans	hot and sunny	go to the beach	dog
Juliette	Angers	cold and rainy	stay home	older sister

6. Describe this person in French using the 3rd person masculine [he]

Name: Paul

Lives in: Mende

Age: 13

Pet: a white dog

Weather: sunny and good weather

Always: goes to the countryside and does hiking

Never: stays at home and does homework

 **THE LANGUAGE GYM**

Grammar Time 13: Jouer, Faire, Aller + Être and Avoir

Jouer to play		
je joue *I play* **tu joues** *you...* **il joue** *he...* **elle joue** *she...* **on joue** *one/we*	**nous jouons** *we play...* **vous jouez** *you guys ...* **ils jouent** *they... masc/**mixed* **elles jouent** *they... all female*	avec des amis au basket aux cartes aux échecs

Faire to do		
je fais **tu fais** **il/elle/on fait**	**nous faisons** **vous faites** **ils/elles font**	du footing de la natation de la randonnée du sport du vélo

Aller to go		
je vais **tu vas** **il/elle/on va**	**nous allons** **vous allez** **ils/elles vont**	en boîte au gymnase au parc à la pêche à la piscine

Être to be		
je suis **tu es** **il/elle/on est**	**nous sommes** **vous êtes** **ils/elles sont**	allemand(e)(s) beau(x)/belle(s) français/française(s) grand(e)(s) petit(e)(s)

Avoir to have		
j'ai **tu as** **il/elle/on a**	**nous avons** **vous avez** **ils/elles ont**	les cheveux châtains un chien et un chat deux frères une grande maison onze ans les yeux noirs

*Author's note: **"Ils" means "they" and should be used for a group of males AND/OR a mixed group of males and females

1. Complete with one of the following verbs: *J'ai – Je fais – Je joue – Je suis – Je vais*

a. _____ du sport   f. _____ un chien   k. _____ du vélo

b. _____ au parc   g. _____ quinze ans   l. _____ aux échecs

c. _____ un chat   h. _____ deux animaux   m. _____ au basket

d. _____ au foot   i. _____ au cinéma   n. _____ les yeux

noirs

---

2. Rewrite the sentences in the first column in the third person singular

je	il , elle
je joue au tennis	
je vais au cinéma	
j'ai un chat	
je suis grande	
je fais de la natation	

4. Complete

a. Je ne v_____ jamais à la piscine.

b. Ma mère ne v____ jamais à l'église.

c. Nous _____ souvent à la plage.

d. Mon frère _____ un chat blanc et noir.

e. Ils s_____anglais, je s_____ italien.

f. Mes parents _____ les cheveux bruns.

g. Mon frère et moi _____ des arts martiaux.

5. Complete with the appropriate verb

a. Je ne _____ jamais au cinéma avec mes parents.

b. Ma sœur et moi _____ au parc.

c. Ma mère _____ quarante ans.

d. Ma cousine _____ très grande et très belle.

e. Mes frères _____ souvent à la Playstation.

f. Il ne _____ jamais de sport, car il est paresseux.

---

3. Translate into English

a. Nous faisons de la natation.

b. Nous jouons aux échecs.

c. Ils ne font pas de natation.

d. Elles vont au cinéma.

e. Nous avons deux chiens.

f. Nous sommes français.

g. Je n'ai pas de sœurs.

h. Je ne suis pas de Paris.

i. Je ne fais rien.

6. Translate into French

a. I never play tennis with him.

b. My mother never goes to church.

c. My brother is tall and slim. He has blond hair and blue eyes.

d. My father is forty years old.

e. My brother goes to the gym every day.

f. They never go to the swimming pool.

Revision Quickie 4: Clothes/Free time/Weather

1. Activities: match up

Je fais mes devoirs	I go to church
Je fais du sport	I go to the swimming pool
Je joue au basket	I go to the gym
Je joue aux cartes	I go window shopping
Je vais à l'église	I do my homework
je vais à la piscine	I go swimming
Je vais au gymnase	I do rock climbing
Je fais du lèche-vitrines	I do sport
Je fais de la natation	I go horse-riding
Je fais de l'équitation	I go to the beach
Je vais à la plage	I play cards
Je fais de l'escalade	I play basketball

2. Weather: complete

a. Il fait fr_ _ _

b. Il fait cha_ _

c. Il y a du sol_ _ _

d. Il ne_ _ _

e. Il fait be_ _

f. Il fait mau_ _ _ _

g. Il y a de l'or_ _ _

h. Il y a du v_ _ _

i. Il pl_ _ _

3. Fill in the gaps in French

a. Quand il fait f_____, je porte un m_____ *When it is cold, I wear a coat*

b. Quand il fait m_____, je _____ à la maison *When the weather is bad, I stay at home*

c. Quand il y a du s_____ , je vais à la p_____ *When it is sunny, I go to the beach*

d. Quand je v_____ au gymnase, je p_____ un s_____
When I go to the gym, I wear a tracksuit

e. Quand il fait c_____, je vais à l___ p_____ *When it is hot, I go to the swimming pool*

f. Le week-end, je f_____ m___ d_____ *At the weekend, I do my homework*

g. Quand j'ai le t_____ , je f_____ de l'e_____
When I have time, I go rock climbing

4. Translate into French

a. When it is hot:

b. When it is cold:

c. I play basketball:

d. I do my homework:

e. I go rock climbing:

f. When I have free time:

g. I go to the swimming pool:

h. I go to the gym:

5. Translate to French

a. I wear a coat:

b. We wear a uniform:

c. They play basketball:

d. She goes rock climbing:

e. He has free time:

f. They go swimming:

g. My parents do sport:

h. She plays football often:

Question Skills 3: Clothes/Free time/Weather

1. Translate into English

a. Que portes-tu quand il fait froid?

b. Quel temps fait-il là où tu habites?

c. Que fais-tu pendant ton temps libre?

d. Tu fais du sport?

e. Tu joues souvent au basket?

f. Pourquoi tu n'aimes pas le foot?

g. Où fais-tu de l'escalade?

h. Quel est ton sport préféré?

2. Complete with the missing question word:

a. _____ habites-tu?

b. _____ sport fais-tu?

c. _____ est ton sport préféré?

d. _____ fais-tu de la natation?

e. _____ achètes-tu tes chaussures?

f. _____ tu n'aimes pas le volley?

g. Avec _____ joues-tu au tennis?

h. _____ tu aimes l'équitation?

i. _____ tu ne joues pas avec moi?

3. Split questions

Que fais-tu	de l'escalade?
Avec qui	fais-tu quand il fait froid?
Pourquoi	pendant ton temps libre?
Où fais-tu	de vêtements?
Que	joues-tu aux échecs?
Quel est	quand il fait chaud?
Tu as beaucoup	ton sport préféré?
Que portes-tu	tu n'aimes pas le tennis?

4. Translate into French

a. What?

b. Where?

c. How?

d. When?

e. Which?

f. How much?

g. How many?

h. From where?

5. Write the questions to these answers

a. Quand il fait froid, je porte un manteau.

b. Je fais du sport le week-end.

c. Je vais au gymnase à cinq heures.

d. J'ai deux survêtements.

e. Je joue au tennis avec mon père ou mon frère.

f. Je fais de la natation dans la piscine près de chez moi.

g. Je fais rarement de l'escalade.

6. Translate into French

a. Where do you play tennis?

b. What do you do when you have free time?

c. How many baseball caps do you have?

d. What is your favourite hobby?

e. Do you do sport often?

f. At what time do you do your homework?

UNIT 16
Talking about my daily routine

In this unit you will learn how to say:

- What you do every day
- At what time you do it
- Sequencing events/actions (e.g. using 'then', 'finally')

You will revisit:
- Numbers
- Free time activities
- Nationalities
- Clothes
- Hair and eyes
- Food
- Jobs

UNIT 16
Talking about my daily routine

		je me brosse les dents *I brush my teeth*	
		je me coiffe *I do my hair*	
Vers... *Around...*		je me couche *I go to bed*	
À... *At*		je déjeune *I have lunch*	
cinq heures *5*		je dîne *I have dinner*	
six heures *6*			
sept heures *7*	**du matin** *in the morning*	je fais mes devoirs *I do my homework*	**ensuite...** *then*
huit heures cinq *8.05*			
huit heures dix *8.10*		je m'habille *I get dressed*	
huit heures et quart *8.15*		je joue sur l'ordinateur *I play on the computer*	
huit heures vingt *8.20*	**de l'après-midi** *in the afternoon*		**après...** *after*
huit heures vingt-cinq *8.25*		je me lève *I get up*	
huit heures et demie *8.30*		je prends le petit-déjeuner *I have breakfast*	
neuf heures moins vingt-cinq *8.35*			**finalement...** *finally*
neuf heures moins vingt *8.40*	**du soir** *in the evening*	je regarde la télé *I watch telly*	
neuf heures moins le quart *8.45*		je rentre à la maison *I go back home*	
neuf heures moins dix *8.50*			
neuf heures moins cinq *8.55*		je me repose *I rest*	
À midi *12pm*		je sors de chez moi *I leave my house*	
À minuit *12am*		je vais au collège en bus *I go to school by bus*	

Unit 16. Talking about my daily routine: VOCAB BUILDING (Part 1)

1. Match up

Je me lève	I have lunch
Je vais au collège	I have dinner
Je me couche	I get up
Je déjeune	I have breakfast
Je dîne	I rest
Je prends le petit-déjeuner	I go to school
Je me repose	I go back home
Je rentre à la maison	I go to bed

2. Translate into English

a. Je me lève à six heures.

b. Je me couche à onze heures.

c. Je déjeune à midi.

d. Je prends le petit-déjeuner à six heures cinq.

e. Je rentre à la maison à trois heures et demie.

f. Je dîne vers huit heures.

g. Je regarde la télé.

h. J'écoute de la musique.

i. Je sors de chez moi à sept heures.

3. Complete with the missing words

a. _____ au collège *I go to school*

b. _____ de chez moi *I leave the house*

c. _____ à la maison *I come back home*

d. _____ la télé *I watch TV*

e. _____ mes devoirs
I do my homework

f. _____ de la musique
I listen to music

g. _____ sur l'ordinateur
I play on the computer

h. _____ à midi *I have lunch at noon*

4. Complete with the missing letters

a. Je me ____pose *I rest*

b. Je ren____ chez moi *I go back home*

c. J'___oute de la musique *I listen to music*

d. Je pr_____ le petit-déjeuner
I have breakfast

e. Je ___ne *I have dinner*

f. Je v_____ au collège *I go to school*

g. Je m___ ____ve *I get up*

h. Je ___e co_____ *I go to bed*

i. Je ___jeune *I have lunch*

5. Faulty translation: spot and correct any mistakes (not all translations are wrong)

a. Je me repose un peu: *I shower a bit*

b. Je me couche à minuit: *I go to bed at noon*

c. Je fais mes devoirs: *I do your homework*

d. Je prends le petit-déjeuner: *I have lunch*

e. Je vais au collège: *I come back from school*

f. Je rentre à la maison: *I leave the house*

g. Je regarde la télé: *I watch TV*

h. Je sors de chez moi: *I leave school*

i. Je me brosse les dents: *I wash my hands*

6. Translate the following times into French

a. At 6.30am:

b. At 7.30am:

c. At 8.20pm:

d. At midday:

e. At 9.20am:

f. At 11.00pm:

g. At midnight:

h. At 5.15pm:

Unit 16. Talking about my daily routine: VOCAB BUILDING (Part 2)

1. Complete the table

Je me couche	
	I brush my teeth
Je me lève	
	I go back home
À huit heures et quart	
Je déjeune	
	I have dinner
J'écoute de la musique	
	I leave the house
Je prends le petit déjeuner	
Je me repose	
	I do my homework
Je m'habille	

2. Complete the sentences using the words in the table below

vingt-cinq	demie	soir	matin	midi
onze	quatre	moins	vers	minuit

a. À sept heures et _____ *At half past seven*

b. _____ cinq heures *At around five o'clock*

c. À huit heures du _____ *At 8 am*

d. À _____ *at noon*

e. À _____ heures et quart *At 11.15*

f. Vers trois heures _____ vingt
At around 2.40

g. À _____ *At midnight*

h. Vers _____ heures *At around four o'clock*

i. Vers neuf heures du _____ *At around 9pm*

j. À cinq heures moins _____
de l'après-midi *At 4.35pm*

3. Translate into English (numerical)

a. À huit heures et demie du matin: At 8.30am

b. À neuf heures et quart du soir: _____

c. À dix heures moins cinq du soir: _____

d. À midi: _____

e. À minuit: _____

f. À onze heures moins cinq du matin: _____

g. À douze heures vingt: _____

h. Vers deux heures de l'après-midi: _____

4. Complete

a. A c_____ h_____ et d_____ *At 5.30*

b. Vers h_____ h_____ et q_____
At around 8.15

c. A m_____ *At noon*

d. A n_____ h_____ m_____ le
q_____ *At 8.45*

e. A m_____ *At midnight*

f. A o_____ h_____ et _____ *At 11.30*

g. Vers u___ h_____ d___ m_____
At around one o'clock in the morning

5. Translate the following into French

a. I go to school at around 8am.

b. I come back home at around 3pm.

c. I have dinner at 7.30pm.

d. I do my homework at around 5.30pm.

e. I have breakfast at 6.45am.

Unit 16. Talking about my daily routine: READING (Part 1)

Je m'appelle Hiroto. Je suis japonais. Ma routine journalière est très simple. En général, je me lève vers six heures. Après, je me douche et je m'habille. Ensuite, je prends le petit-déjeuner avec ma mère et mon petit frère. Après, je me brosse les dents et je me coiffe. Vers sept heures et demie, je sors de chez moi et je vais au collège en vélo. Je rentre à la maison vers quatre heures. Après, je me repose un peu. En général, je regarde la télé. Ensuite, je vais au parc avec mes amis jusqu'à six heures. De six heures à sept heures et demie, je fais mes devoirs. A huit heures, je dîne avec ma famille. Je ne mange pas beaucoup, juste un sandwich au jambon. Finalement, je regarde un film et je me couche vers onze heures.

Je m'appelle Gregorio. Je suis mexicain. En général, je me lève à sept heures et quart. Après, je me douche et je prends le petit-déjeuner avec mes deux frères. Ensuite, je me brosse les dents et je prépare mon sac. Vers sept heures, je vais au collège à pied. Je rentre chez moi vers trois heures et demie. Après, je me détends un peu. En général, je surfe sur internet, je regarde une série sur Netflix ou je tchatte avec mes amis sur Whatsapp. De cinq à six heures, je fais mes devoirs. Vers sept heures et demie, je dîne avec ma famille. Je mange du riz ou une salade. Finalement, je regarde la télé et je me couche vers dix heures.

Je m'appelle Andreas. Je suis allemand. Ma routine journalière est très simple. Généralement, je me lève tôt, vers cinq heures. Je fais du footing, je me douche et je m'habille. Ensuite, vers six heures et demie je prends le petit-déjeuner avec ma mère et ma sœur. Je mange des fuits et je bois un chocolat chaud. Après, je me brosse les dents et je prépare mon sac. Vers sept heures et quart, je sors de chez moi et je vais au collège. Je rentre chez moi vers trois heures et demie. Après, je me repose un peu. Normalement, je regarde la télé ou je tchatte avec mes amis sur internet. De six à huit heures, je fais mes devoirs. Je dîne avec ma famille à huit heures. Finalement, je joue à la Playstation jusqu'à minuit et je me couche.

1. Answer the following questions about Hiroto

a. Where is he from?

b. At what time does he get up?

c. Who does he have breakfast with?

d. At what time does he leave the house?

e. Until what time does he stay at the park?

f. How does he go to school?

2. Find the French for the phrases below in Hiroto's text

a. At around eleven

b. With my friends

c. I go by bike

d. I go to the park

e. I shower and get dressed

f. I don't eat much

g. From six to half seven

h. I do my homework

3. Complete the statements below about Andreas' text

a. He gets up at _____.

b. He comes back from school at _____.

c. For breakfast he eats _____ and drinks a _____ _____.

d. He has breakfast with _____.

e. After getting up he _____, then showers and _____.

f. Usually he _____ until midnight.

4. Find the French for the following phrases/sentences in Gregorio's text

a. I am Mexican

b. I shower

c. With my two brothers

d. I relax a bit

Unit 16. Talking about my daily routine: READING (Part 2)

Je m'appelle Yang. J'ai douze ans et je suis chinoise. Ma routine journalière est très simple. Généralement, je me lève vers six heures et demie. Après je me douche et je m'habille. Ensuite, je prends le petit-déjeuner avec ma mère et mon frère, Li Wei. Je ne mange pas beaucoup le matin. Ensuite, je me brosse les dents et je prépare mon sac. Vers sept heures et demie, je sors de chez moi et je vais au collège. Je rentre à la maison vers quatre heures. Après, je me détends un peu. Normalement, je regarde la télé, j'écoute de la musique ou je lis mes bandes dessinées préférées. De six à sept heures et demie, je fais mes devoirs. Ensuite, je dîne avec ma famille, je regarde un film et je me couche vers onze heures.

Je m'appelle Anna et je suis italienne. En général, je me lève à six heures et quart. Ensuite, je me lave et je prends le petit-déjeuner avec ma sœur aînée. Vers sept heures, je vais au collège en bus. Je rentre chez moi vers deux heures et demie et je me repose un peu. D'habitude, je surfe sur internet, je regarde la télé ou je lis des revues de mode. De cinq à sept heures, je fais mon travail scolaire. À huit heures, je dîne avec ma famille. Je mange des fruits ou une salade. Finalement, je lis un roman et vers onze heures, je me couche.

Je m'appelle Kim, je suis anglaise. J'ai quinze ans. Généralement, je me lève tôt, vers cinq heures et demie. Je fais un footing, je me lave et je m'habille. Après, vers sept heures, je prends le petit-déjeuner avec ma mère et ma demi-sœur. Ensuite, je me brosse les dents et je prépare mon sac. Vers sept heures et demie, je sors de chez moi et je vais au collège. Je rentre à la maison vers trois heures. Après, je me détends un peu. Normalement, j'écoute de la musique ou je tchatte avec mes amis sur internet puis de six à huit heures, je fais mes devoirs. À huit heures et quart, je dîne avec ma famille. Finalement, je regarde un film à la télé jusqu'à minuit et je me couche.

1. Find the French for the following in Yang's text

a. I am Chinese

b. My daily routine

c. I shower

d. Very simple

e. At around 7.30

f. I don't eat much

g. I watch telly

h. I go to school

i. I do my homework

j. From six to seven thirty

k. I watch a movie

2. Translate these items from Kim's text

a. I am English

b. Generally

c. around 5.30

d. With my mum and stepsister

e. I go back home

f. At around three

g. I have dinner with my family

h. I rest a bit

i. I brush my teeth

3. Answer the following questions on Anna's text

a. What nationality is Anna?

b. At what time does she get up?

c. What three things does she do after school?

d. How does she go to school?

e. Who does she have breakfast with?

f. At what time does she go to bed?

g. What does she eat for dinner?

h. What does she read before going to bed?

4. Find someone who…

a. has breakfast with their older sister

b. doesn't watch telly at night

c. reads fashion magazines

d. gets up at 5.30am

e. has breakfast with their brother and mother

f. chats with their friends on the internet after school

g. does exercise in the morning

Unit 16. Talking about my daily routine: WRITING

1. Split sentences

Je vais au collège	chez moi
Je rentre	devoirs
Je fais mes	en bus
Je regarde	la télé
Je joue sur	à minuit
Je me lève	à la maison
Je me couche	vers six heures
Je sors de	l'ordinateur

2. Complete with the correct option

a. Je me lève à _____ heures du matin.

b. Je fais _____ devoirs.

c. Je regarde _____ télé.

d. Je joue sur mon _____.

e. Je me _____ à minuit.

f. Je rentre _____ maison.

g. Je sors de _____ moi.

h. Je vais au collège _____ bus.

à la	couche	six	en
la	mes	chez	ordinateur

3. Spot and correct the grammar and spelling mistakes in several cases a word is missing

a. Je vais collège en vélo.

b. Je me lève à sept heures et demi.

c. Je sors chez moi à huit heures.

d. Je rentre au maison.

e. Je vais collège en bus.

f. Je me couche vers onze.

g. Je dîne à huit heures moins le quarter.

h. Je fais mes devoirs à cinq heures demie.

4. Complete the words

a. Qu_____ *Quarter*

b. De_____ *Half*

c. À d___ h_____ *At 10*

d. V___ n____ h_____ *At around 9*

e. À h_____ h_____ *At 8*

f. Vi_____ *Twenty*

g. E_____ *Then*

h. Je _____ *I have lunch*

i. Je _____ *I come back*

j. Je _____ *I play*

5. Guided writing: write 3 short paragraphs in the first person I using the details below

Person	Gets up	Showers	Goes to school	Comes back home	Watches telly	Has dinner	Goes to bed
Éloi	6.30	7.00	8.05	3.30	6.00	8.10	11.10
Sandrine	6.40	7.10	7.40	4.00	6.30	8.15	12.00
Juliette	7.15	7.30	8.00	3.15	6.40	8.20	11.30

Revision Quickie 5: Clothes / Food / Free Time / Describing people

1. Clothes: match up

Une écharpe (1)	A baseball cap
Un survêtement	A skirt
Une casquette	A dress
Une cravate	A shirt
Une jupe	A T-shirt
Une robe	Jeans
Un tee-shirt	A tracksuit
Une chemise	Socks
Un jean	Trousers
Des chaussettes	A scarf (1)
Un pantalon	A tie

3. Complete the translations below

a. Shoes : *Chau_____*

b. Hat: *Cha_____*

c. Hair: *Ch_____*

d. Curly: *Fr_____*

e. Purple: *Vio_____*

f. Milk: *La_____*

g. Water: *E_____*

h. Drink: *Bo_____*

i. Job: *Tr_____*

j. Clothes: *Vê_____*

5. Match questions and answers

Quel est ton travail préféré?	Un survêtement
Quelle est ta couleur préférée?	Mon professeur de dessin
Quelle viande détestes-tu?	Docteur
Que portes-tu en général pour aller au gymnase?	Les échecs
Qui est ton prof préféré?	Le bleu
Quelle est ta boisson préférée?	Le porc
Quel est ton passe-temps préféré?	Le jus de fruits

2. Food: provide a word for each of the cues below

A fruit starting with **P**	La pomme
A vegetable starting with **C**	
A dairy product starting with **F**	
A meat starting with **B**	
A drink starting with **J**	
A drink made using lemons **L**	
A sweet dessert starting with **G**	
A fruit starting with **F**	

4. Clothes, Colours, Food, Jobs: categories

Vêtements	Couleurs	Travail	Nourriture

chemise	bleu	comptable	plombier
viande	rose	avocat	poulet
costume	cuisinier	fromage	cravate
orange	chapeau	riz	rouge

6. Free time: complete with *fais, joue or vais* as appropriate

a. Je ne _____ pas de sport.

b. Je ne _____ jamais au basket.

c. Je _____ souvent au gymnase.

d. Je _____ du vélo tous les jours.

e. Je _____ souvent à la Playstation.

f. Je ne _____ pas à la piscine aujourd'hui.

THE LANGUAGE GYM

135

7. Complete with the missing verb, choosing from the list below

a. Je _____ beaucoup de jus de fruits.

b. J' _____ les fraises.

c. Après avoir fait mes devoirs, je _____ au gymnase ou je _____ aux jeux vidéo.

d. Je _____ beaucoup de sport.

e. Le matin, je ne _____ pas beaucoup. Seulement deux tartines avec du miel.

f. Mon père _____ comme ingénieur. Je ne _____ pas encore. Je_____ étudiant.

g. Je _____ regarder des dessins animés. Je _____ regarder des séries sur Netflix.

h. Le matin, je me _____ vers six heures.

lève	joue	aime	travaille
vais	fais	préfère	suis
travaille	bois	déteste	mange

11. Translate into French
a. I play tennis every day.

b. I wear a jacket sometimes.

c. I go to the gym often.

d. I don't watch cartoons.

e. I get up at around 6am.

f. I shower twice a day.

g. I go to bed at midnight.

8. Time markers: translate

a. Jamais:

b. De temps en temps:

c. Toujours:

d. Tous les jours:

e. Rarement:

f. Une fois par semaine:

g. Deux fois par mois:

h. Tous les matins:

9. Split sentences (Relationships)

Je m'entends bien	mes grands-parents
Je ne m'entends pas	avec ma mère
Mes parents	grand et fort
J'adore	bien avec mon père
Mon frère est	de dessin est strict
Mon professeur	sont généreux
Ma petite amie est	car il est méchant
Je déteste mon oncle	belle
Je ne supporte pas	cousins
J'adore mes	ma sœur

10. Complete the translation

a. Mon frère est _____.
My brother is a fireman.

b. Je ne _____ pas, je suis _____. *I don't work, I am a student.*

c. De temps en temps, je _____ au cinéma avec mon père. *From time to time I go to the cinema with my father.*

d. Je ne _____ jamais la télé. *I never watch tv.*

e. Je _____ mes professeurs. *I hate my teachers.*

f. Mes parents sont _____. *My parents are strict.*

g. Je _____ du footing tous les jours. *I go jogging every day.*

UNIT 17
Describing my house:
- indicating where it is located
- saying what I like/dislike about it

In this unit you will learn how to say in French

- Where your house/apartment is located
- What your favourite room is
- What you like to do in each room
- The present indicative of key reflexive verbs in -ER

You will revisit:
- Adjectives to describe places
- Frequency markers
- Countries

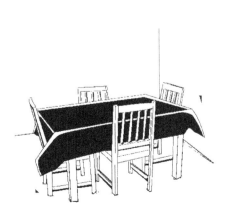

UNIT 17
Describing my house

J'habite dans une *I live in a*	**jolie** *pretty* **grande** *big* **petite** *small* **vieille** *old*	**maison**	**dans la banlieue** *on the outskirts* **à la campagne** *in the countryside* **au/en centre-ville** *in the city centre*
J'habite dans un *I live in a*	**joli** *beautiful* **grand** *big* **petit** *small* **vieil** *old*	**appartement**	**sur la côte** *on the coast* **à la montagne** *in the mountain* **dans un quartier résidentiel** *in a residential neighbourhood*

Dans ma maison, il y a quatre/cinq/six pièces *In my house there are 4/5/6 rooms*	
Ma pièce favorite est… *My favourite room is*	**ma chambre** *my bedroom*
J'aime me détendre dans… *I like to relax in*	**la cuisine** *the kitchen* **le jardin** *the garden*
J'aime me reposer dans… *I like to rest in*	**la salle de bain** *the bathroom* **la salle à manger** *the dining room*
J'aime travailler dans… *I like to work in*	**le salon** *the living room*
Je me douche toujours dans… *I always shower in*	**la terrasse** *the terrace*

THE LANGUAGE GYM

Unit 17. Describing my house: VOCABULARY BUILDING PART 1

1. Match up

J'habite dans	A flat
Une maison	New
Un appartement	Residential
Grand	Neighbourhood
Neuf	I live in
La campagne	A house
Quartier	Big
Résidentiel	The countryside

2. Translate into English

a. J'habite dans une petite et vieille maison.

b. J'habite dans un grand appartement.

c. Mon appartement est dans la banlieue.

d. Ma maison est à la campagne.

e. Ma pièce favorite est ma chambre.

f. J'aime la cuisine.

g. J'aime travailler dans le salon.

h. Je me douche toujours dans la salle de bain.

i. J'aime me reposer dans le jardin.

3. Complete with the missing words

a. J'habite ____ la côte. *I live on the coast.*

b. J'_____ ma maison. *I like my house.*

c. _____ dans une vieille, mais _____ maison. *I live in an old but pretty house.*

d. J'aime _____ dans le salon. *I like to relax in the living room.*

e. Ma _____ est dans la _____.

My house is on the outskirts.

f. Je ne me _____ jamais dans le jardin! *I never shower in the garden!*

g. J'_____ lire sur la terrasse. *I love reading on the terrace.*

4. Complete the words

a. Une v_____ m_____ *An old house*

b. Un _____ sur la c_____
A flat on the coast

c. Une _____ m_____ *A small house*

d. Une _____ t_____ *A big terrace*

e. Une _____ c_____ *A pretty bedroom*

f. Dans la b_____ *On the outskirts*

5. Classify the words/phrases below in the table below

a. toujours	i. grande
b. je me repose	j. parfois
c. jamais	k. salle à manger
d. joli	l. campagne
e. vieille	m. petit
f. montagne	n. travailler
g. je me douche	o. côte
h. chambre	p. j'habite

Time phrases	Nouns	Verbs	Adjectives
a.			

6. Translate into French

a. I live in an old flat.

b. I live in a new house.

c. In the town centre.

d. I like to relax in the living room.

e. I always shower in the bathroom.

f. I live in a residential neighbourhood.

g. My favourite room is the kitchen.

Unit 17. Describing my house: VOCABULARY BUILDING PART 2

1. Match up

J'habite dans	côte
Une jolie	résidentiel
Sur la	un appartement
Un appartement	maison
Dans le	moderne
Un quartier	toujours
Je me repose	centre-ville
J'aime	ma chambre

2. Complete with the missing word

a. Je n'aime pas _____ *I don't like to work*

b. Elle est petite, mais _____ *It is small, but pretty*

c. C'est dans le _____- _____ *It is in the town centre*

d. C'est dans la _____ *It is on the outskirts*

e. J'habite dans une grande _____
I live in a big house

f. Dans un _____ résidentiel
in a residential neighbourhood

g. Ma _____ favorite est… *My favourite room is...*

h. Je me repose dans le _____
I rest in the garden

i. J'étudie dans ma _____ *I study in my bedroom*

3. Translate into English

a. Je vis dans une petite maison.

b. C'est sur la côte.

c. Un grand appartement.

d. C'est dans un quartier résidentiel.

e. Chez moi, il y a cinq pièces.

f. J'aime travailler dans la salle à manger.

g. J'aime me reposer.

h. Je vis en centre-ville.

i. J'habite dans la banlieue.

4. Broken words

a. J'aime me re_____ *I like to rest*

b. Je vis à la m_____
I live in the mountain

c. Dans le centre-_____ *the town centre*

d. Je ne me d_____ jamais... *I never shower...*

e. …dans le j_____ ...*in the garden*

f. Ma pièce f_____ … *my favourite room is...*

g. Ma ch_____ *my bedroom*

5. 'Le' or 'La'?

a. __LA__ côte

b. _____ campagne

c. _____ salle à manger

d. _____ salon

e. _____ ville

f. _____ jardin

g. _____ salle de bain

h. _____ chambre

i. _____ banlieue

j. _____ quartier

6. Bad translation – spot any translation errors and fix them

a. J'habite dans une maison sur la côte.

I live in a flat on the coast.

b. Ma pièce favorite est la cuisine.

My favourite room is the dining room.

c. J'aime me détendre dans ma chambre.

I like to work in my bedroom.

d. J'habite dans un appartement dans un quartier résidentiel.

I live in a house in a residential neighbourhood.

e. J'aime ma maison car elle est grande et jolie.

I don't like my house because it is big and ugly.

f. J'aime lire dans le salon. *I like to work in the kitchen.*

 THE LANGUAGE GYM

Unit 17. Describing my house: READING

Je m'appelle Dante. Je suis d'Italie. Je vis dans une très grande maison sur la côte. J'aime beaucoup cela. Dans ma maison, il y a dix pièces et ma pièce favorite, c'est la cuisine. J'aime cuisiner *(to cook)* dans la cuisine avec ma mère. Généralement je me lève, je me douche dans la salle de bain et après je m'habille dans ma chambre. Mon ami Paolo habite dans une petite maison à la montagne. Paolo est très amusant et travailleur. Il n'aime pas sa maison car elle est trop *(too)* petite.

Je m'appelle Monica. Je suis italienne et je vis dans une très vieille, mais très jolie maison à la campagne en Italie. J'adore ma maison! Chez moi, il y a cinq pièces, mais ma pièce favorite c'est le salon. Tous les jours, après le collège, j'aime me reposer dans le salon et regarder la télé avec ma sœur. Je n'aime pas la salle de bain car parfois il y a des souris.

Je m'appelle Ariella. Je suis de Cuba. Je me lève toujours à cinq heures du matin car je vis loin du collège, dans la banlieue de ma ville. J'habite dans un appartement dans un bâtiment ancien. L'appartement est très vieux et un peu moche, mais je l'aime bien. J'aime me reposer dans ma chambre. Parfois je lis des livres ou j'écoute de la musique sur Spotify. Ma chambre est ma pièce préférée.

Je m'appelle Michel et je suis de Biarritz, au Pays basque. Ma maison est en centre-ville et je vis près de la côte. Chez moi, je parle basque et français; le basque est une langue très ancienne. Je vis dans une petite maison neuve et très jolie. Il y a six pièces et j'ai aussi un grand jardin. Mon cheval vit dans le jardin. Il s'appelle Dingo. Dans ma maison, ma pièce favorite, c'est la salle à manger car j'adore manger!

J'aime me reposer dans ma chambre. Je regarde toujours des dessins animés et des séries sur Netflix. J'aime aussi travailler là, quand je fais mes devoirs par exemple.

1. Answer the following questions about Dante

a. Where is he from?

b. What is his house like?

c. How many rooms are there in his house?

d. Which is his favourite room?

e. Where does he get dressed?

f. Where does Paolo live?

g. Does Paolo like his house? (Why?)

2. Find the French for the phrases below in Michel's text

a. My house is in the centre

b. I live near…

c. I speak Basque

d. I also have a big garden

e. I love eating

f. He lives in the garden

g. I like to rest

h. I also like to work there

3. Find Someone Who…

a. lives far from school

b. speaks two languages

c. has a really really big house

d. sometimes finds 'unwanted guests' in the bathroom

e. has a big pet that lives outside the house

f. listens to music on a streaming platform

g. is a foodie (loves food)

h. has a friend that doesn't like their house

4. Find the French for the following phrases/sentences in Ariella's text

a. I am from Cuba

b. I always wake up at 5

c. I live far from school

d. The flat is very old

e. And a bit ugly

f. But I like it

g. Sometimes I read books

Unit 17. Describing my house: TRANSLATION

1. Gapped translation

a. J'habite dans la banlieue. *I live on the_____.*

b. Ma maison est très jolie, mais un peu petite.

My house is _____ pretty, but ___ _____ small.

c. C'est à la montagne. *It is in the _____.*

d. Je vis dans le _____-_____.

I live in the city centre.

e. Dans ma maison, ___ ___ ___ cinq pièces.

In my house, there are five rooms.

f. Je n'aime pas beaucoup la _____, car elle est _____.

I don't really like the kitchen, because it's ugly.

2. Translate to English

a. La côte:

b. Un appartement:

c. J'habite dans:

d. Le centre-ville:

e. Ma pièce favorite:

f. J'aime me reposer:

g. La chambre:

h. Le salon:

3. Translate into English

a. J'habite dans un petit appartement moche.

b. Ma maison est moderne, mais assez jolie.

c. Mon appartement est vieux, mais je l'aime beaucoup.

d. Je vis dans une maison sur la côte.

e. Dans ma maison, il y a cinq pièces.

f. Ma pièce favorite, c'est ma chambre.

4. Translate into French

a. Big: G

b. Small: P

c. Outskirts: B

d. Coast: C

e. Neighbourhood: Q

f. Residential: R

g. Ugly: M

h. Room: P

i. There are: I

j. Old (f): V

5. Translate into French

a. I live in a small house

b. In the city centre

c. In my house there are…

d. Seven rooms

e. My favourite room is...

f. The living room

g. I like to relax in my bedroom

h. And I like to work in the living room

i. I live in a small and old flat

j. In a residential neighbourhood

Grammar Time 14: HABITER – to live

J'habite *I live* **Tu habites** *You* **Il habite** *He* **Elle habite** *She* **Nous habitons** *We* **Vous habitez** *You guys* **Ils habitent** *They - masculine/mixed* **Elles habitent** *They -female*	**dans une maison**	**ancienne** *old* **confortable** *comfortable* **contemporaine** *contemporary* **minuscule** *tiny* **moche** *ugly* **moderne** *modern* **neuve** *new* **spacieuse** *spacious*	**dans la banlieue** *on the outskirts* **à la campagne** *in the countryside* **au/en centre-ville** *in the city centre* **sur la côte** *on the coast* **à la montagne** *in the mountains* **dans un quartier résidentiel** *in a residential neighbourhood*
	dans un appartement	**ancien** *old* **confortable** *comfortable* **contemporain** *contemporary* **minuscule** *tiny* **moche** *ugly* **moderne** *modern* **neuf** *new* **spacieux** *spacious*	

AUTHOR'S NOTE

'Habiter' can be swapped at any time with the verb 'vivre' (to live)

-Je vis: *I live*

-Tu vis: *you live*

-Il/elle/on vit: *he/she/one lives*

-Nous vivons: *we live*

-Vous vivez: *you guys live*

-Il/elles vivent: *they live*

1. Match

Ils habitent	I live
Nous habitons	You live
Elle habite	She lives
J'habite	We live
Vous habitez	You guys live
Tu habites	They live

2. Complete with the correct form of 'habiter'

a. J' _____ dans une jolie maison.

I live in a beautiful house.

b. Où _____-tu? *Where do you live?*

c. Nous _____ à Londres depuis trois ans.

We have been living in London for three years.

d. _____ dans une maison sur la côte.

She lives in a house on the coast.

e. Tu _____ dans une maison ou un

appartement? *Do you live in a house or in a flat?*

f. Ils _____ dans un appartement ancien.

They live in an old flat.

g. Nous _____ dans la banlieue.

We live on the outskirts.

h. Mon père _____ dans une ferme.

My father lives on a farm.

3. Complete with the correct form of 'vivre'

a. Ma mère et moi _____ à

Biarritz. Mon père _____ à Paris.

b. Où _____-vous?

c. Je _____ à Londres. Mon frère

_____ à Rome.

d. Mes oncles _____ aux

États-Unis.

e. Ma petite amie ne _____ pas ici.

f. Je _____ dans une très grande

maison dans la banlieue.

4. Spot and correct the errors

a. Je ne habitons pas en centre-ville.

b. Mes parents habitez ici.

c. Ma petite amie habitent dans une maison moderne.

d. Ma mère et moi habitez dans la banlieue.

e. Mes frères ne habite pas avec nous.

f. Ma grand-mère maternelle vis avec nous.

5. Complete the translation with 'habiter'

a. *My brothers live in the countryside:*

Mes _____ _____ à la

_____

b. *I live in a flat:* _____ dans un

_____

c. *My mother doesn't live with my father:*

Ma mère n' _____ _____ avec mon père

d. *We live on the outskirts:*

Nous _____ dans la _____

e. *Where do you live?* Où _____-tu?

6. Translate into French (use habiter)

a. My parents and I live in a comfortable house.

b. My mother lives in a small house on the coast.

c. My cousins live in a beautiful house in the countryside.

d. My girlfriend lives in a modern flat in the centre.

e. My sisters live in an old flat on the ouskirts.

f. My best friend Paul lives in a spacious flat near the town centre.

 **THE LANGUAGE GYM**

Grammar Time 15: Reflexives (Part 1)

USEFUL VOCABULARY

S'appeler	To be called
Se baigner	To bathe
Se brosser les dents	To brush one's teeth
Se doucher	To shower
Se laver	To wash
Se lever	To get up
Se raser	To shave
Se reposer	To rest
Se peigner	To comb one's hair
Se préparer	To get ready

Present Indicative of ER reflexive verbs

	se laver	se doucher
je	me lave	me douche
tu	te laves	te douches
il **elle** **on**	se lave	se douche
nous	nous lavons	nous douchons
vous	vous lavez	vous douchez
ils **elles**	se lavent	se douchent

1. Complete with <u>me</u>, <u>se</u> or <u>nous</u>

a. Elles _____ lèvent

b. Je _____ douche

c. Elle _____ repose

d. Nous _____ lavons

e. Il _____ brosse les dents

f. Nous _____ peignons

g. Elles _____ reposent

h. Ils _____ préparent

2. Complete with the correct form of the verb

a. (elles – se brosser) _____ _____ _____ les dents

b. (nous – se doucher) _____ _____ _____ ensuite

c. (il – se fatiguer) _____ _____ _____ beaucoup pendant les cours d'éducation physique

d. (il – se raser) _____ ne _____ _____ jamais

e. (elle – se reposer) _____ ne _____ _____ jamais

f. (ils – se lever) _____ _____ _____ tôt

g. (il – se baigner) ____ ____ _____ toujours dans la mer

3. Translate into English

a. Je me lève vers six heures, mais mon frère se lève vers sept heures. Je me douche ensuite. Mon frère ne se douche jamais.

b. Ma sœur se prépare avant d'aller au collège. Elle se regarde toujours dans le miroir.

c. Je me rase presque *(nearly)* tous les jours. Mon père se rase une fois par semaine.

d. Mes parents se lèvent plus tôt que moi. Après, ils se lavent et prennent le petit-déjeuner avant moi.

e. Mon père est chauve, donc il ne se peigne jamais.

f. Ma mère a beaucoup de cheveux. Elle se peigne pendant une demie heure avant de sortir de la maison.

g. Je me brosse les dents cinq fois par jour. Nous n'avons pas de baignoire chez moi. Ainsi, nous nous douchons tout le temps.

h. Par contre, mon frère ne se brosse les dents qu'une seule fois par jour.

Je me lève après mon père, une demie heure plus tard, vers six heures et demie. Je me douche, je me lave les cheveux, je me rase, je me peigne et pour finir, je m'habille avant d'aller dans la cuisine. Je prends le petit-déjeuner seul. Je mange des céréales avec du lait, des tartines avec de la confiture et je bois un café au lait. Ensuite, je me brosse les dents, je me prépare pour aller au collège et vers sept heures et quart, je sors de chez moi. (Martin, 14)

5. Find the French in Martin's text

a. I get up:

b. I wash:

c. I comb my hair:

d. I brush my teeth:

e. I get ready:

f. I shave:

g. I shower:

h. I drink:

i. I leave the house:

6. Complete

a. Je me douch___   *I shower*

b. Il se ras___   *He shaves*

c. Nous nous douch___ ___ ___   *We shower*

d. Vous vous lav___ ___   *You guys wash*

e. Je me prépar___   *I get ready*

f. Ils se peign___ ___ ___   *They comb their hair*

g. Je me bross___ les dents   *I brush my teeth*

h. Elles se baign___ ___ ___   *They bathe*

8. Translate

a. Normally, I shower at seven o'clock.

b. He never brushes his teeth.

c. We shave three times a week.

d. They get up early.

e. He never combs his hair.

f. I bathe once a week.

g. We prepare ourselves for school.

h. They never relax.

4. Find the French in Philippe's text (below):

a. They get up:

b. My father gets up:

c. He showers:

d. She drinks a coffee:

e. My mother gets up:

f. He leaves the house:

g. He shaves:

h. He combs his hair:

Mes parents se lèvent très tôt. Ma mère se lève vers cinq heures et demie, pour préparer le petit-déjeuner pour mon père et pour nous. Avant de préparer le petit-déjeuner, elle se douche, elle s'habille et elle boit un café en regardant la télé. Mon père se lève une demie heure plus tard. Il se douche, se rase, se peigne, s'habille et après il prend le petit-déjeuner avec ma mère dans la cuisine. Il sort de la maison une demie heure plus tard, vers sept heures. (Philippe, 12)

7. Complete

a. _____ ____ _____ à six heures. *They (fem) get up at six.*

b. _____ ____ _____ à sept heures. *They (masc) shave at seven.*

c. _____ ____ _____ tôt. *I get up early.*

d. Je _____ _____ _____ jamais. *I never shave.*

e. Nous _____ _____ les dents après manger. *We brush our teeth after eating.*

f. Elle_____ _____ toujours dans le miroir. *She always looks at herself in the mirror.*

 THE LANGUAGE GYM

UNIT 18
Saying what I do at home, how often, when and where

In this unit you will learn how to provide a more detailed account of your daily activities building on the vocabulary learnt in the previous unit.

You will revisit:
- Time markers
- Reflexive verbs
- Parts of the house
- Description of people and places
- Telling the time
- Nationalities
- The verbs 'faire', 'jouer' and 'aller'

Unit 18
Saying what I do at home, how often, when and where

D'habitude *Usually*	**je me brosse les dents** *I brush my teeth*	
	je discute avec ma mère	**dans la chambre de mon frère**
	I chat with my mum	*in my brother's bedroom*
Deux fois par semaine *Twice a week*	**j'écoute de la musique** *I listen to music*	**dans la chambre de mes parents**
	je fais mes devoirs *I do my homework*	*in my parents' bedroom*
	je fais du vélo *I ride my bike*	
Normalement *Normally*	**je m'habille** *I get dressed*	**dans ma chambre** *in my bedroom*
	je joue à la Playstation *I play Playstation*	
Parfois *Sometimes*	**je me lave les dents** *I brush my teeth*	**dans la cuisine** *in the kitchen*
	je lis des bandes dessinées *I read comics*	
Quand j'ai le temps *When I have time*	**je lis des magazines** *I read magazines*	**dans le garage** *in the garage*
	je prends le petit-déjeuner *I have breakfast*	**dans le jardin** *in the garden*
Souvent *Often*	**je prépare le repas** *I prepare food*	**dans la salle de bain** *in the bathroom*
Tous les jours *Every day*	**je poste des photos sur Instagram** *I post photos on Instagram*	**dans la salle de jeux** *in the game room*
Trois fois par mois *Three times a month*	**je regarde la télé** *I watch TV*	**dans la salle à manger** *in the dining room*
	je regarde des films *I watch films*	
Vers six, sept, huit… du matin *At around 6,7,8am…*	**je regarde des séries sur Netflix** *I watch series on Netflix*	**dans le salon** *in the living room*
	je me repose *I rest*	**sur la terrasse** *on the terrace*
	je sors de chez moi *I leave the house*	
	je surfe sur internet *I surf on the internet*	

Unit 18. Saying what I do at home: VOCABULARY BUILDING PART 1

1. Match up

Je lis des magazines	I chat with
Je regarde des films	I wash
Je prépare le repas	I watch movies
Je lis des romans	I prepare food
Je m'habille	I read magazines
Je discute avec	I shower
Je me lave	I get dressed
Je me douche	I read novels

2. Complete with the missing words

a. Je m'_____ : *I get dressed*

b. Je lis des _____ : *I read novels*

c. Je lis des _____ :

I read magazines

d. Je me brosse les _____ :

I brush my teeth

e. Je me _____ : *I shower*

f. _____ le repas:

I prepare food

g. Je _____ sur internet:

I surf on the internet

3. Translate into English

a. Généralement, je me douche vers sept heures du matin.

b. Je ne prépare jamais le repas.

c. En général, je lis des magazines dans le salon.

d. Vers sept heures et quart, je prends mon petit-déjeuner dans la salle à manger.

e. De temps en temps, je discute avec ma mère dans la cuisine.

f. Parfois, je prends mon petit-déjeuner dans la cuisine.

g. Je joue tous les jours à la Playstation avec mon frère dans la salle de jeux.

4. Complete the words

a. Je me d_____ *I shower*   g. Je v_____ *I go*

b. Je _____ *I read*   h. Je_____ *I play*

c. Je d_____ *I chat*   i. Je _____ *I leave*

d. Je p_____ *I prepare*   j. Je_____ *I do*

e. J'_____ *I listen*   k. Je_____ *I surf*

f. Je me l_____ *I wash*

5. Classify the words/phrases below in the table below

a. vers six heures	i. je me brosse les dents
b. toujours	j. parfois
c. jamais	k. tous les jours
d. ma chambre	l. j'écoute de la musique
e. je regarde la télé	m. je lis des magazines
f. je joue sur mon ordinateur	n. je fais du vélo
g. je me lave	o. deux fois par semaine
h. je poste des photos sur IG	p. je tchatte sur Skype

Time phrases	Rooms in the house	Things you do in the bathroom	Free-time activities
a.			

6. Fill in the table with what activities you do in which room

Je joue à la Playstation	Dans ma chambre
Je regarde la télé	
Je me douche	
Je fais mes devoirs	
Je me brosse les dents	
Je me repose	

 **THE LANGUAGE GYM**

Unit 18. Saying what I do at home: VOCABULARY BUILDING PART 2

7. Complete the table

English	Français
I get dressed	
I shower	
	Je fais mes devoirs
I upload photos	
	Je sors de chez moi
	Je discute avec mon frère
I rest	

8. Multiple choice quiz

	A	B	C
Jamais	always	never	sometimes
Parfois	sometimes	always	never
Chambre	bedroom	lounge	garden
Je me lave	I shave	I wash	I go out
Je me douche	I shower	I go out	I rest
Je me repose	I go out	I watch	I rest
Jardin	garden	garage	kitchen
Cuisine	bedroom	lounge	kitchen
Je joue	I rest	I play	I prepare
Je lis	I watch	I read	I play
Je sors	I go out	I rest	I read
Toujours	always	never	every day

9. Anagrams

Jiamas: *jamais = never*

siCiune:

breCham:

loSna:

Toursjou:

enuvoSt:

10. Broken words

a. La cu_____ : *Kitchen*

b. Jam_____ : *Never*

c. Par_____ : *Sometimes*

d. Tou_____ : *Always*

e. Sou_____ : *Often*

f. Les ba_____ _____ : *Comics*

g. Ma ch_____ : *My bedroom*

h. Je s_____ : *I go out*

11. Complete based on the translation in brackets

a. Vers s_____ h_____ et demie, je m___
b_____ l____ d_____.
Around seven thirty, I brush my teeth.

b. V_____ d_____ h_____ et quart, je
d_____. *Around quarter past twelve I have lunch.*

c. Par_____, je p_____ l____
r_____. *Sometimes, I prepare the food.*

d. Je r_____ t_____ l____
t_____ quand je p_____ mon p_____-
_____. *I always watch telly when I have
my breakfast.*

e. G_____, je s_____ d____
c_____ m_____ à h_____ h_____ et
demie. *Generally, I leave the house at eight thirty.*

f. Je l_____ r_____ des b_____
d_____. *I read comics rarely.*

12. Gap-fill from memory

a. Parfois, je _____ des magazines.

b. Je me _____ toujours les
dents après manger.

c. Je _____ des séries
sur Netflix tous les soirs.

d. Je ne _____ pas de revues de
mode.

e. Je ne _____ jamais mes devoirs.

f. Je _____ souvent des photos
sur Instagram.

g. Le week-end, je _____ du vélo.

h. Je _____ de chez moi vers
huit heures et quart.

Unit 18. Saying what I do at home: READING

Je m'appelle Fabien. Je suis de Gibraltar. J'ai un chien chez moi. Je me lève toujours tôt, à cinq heures et quart. Après, je vais au gymnase et je fais du sport. Je me douche quand je rentre chez moi. Mon frère Joël est très paresseux. Il se lève à sept heures. Joël ne joue jamais au foot et il ne fait jamais de sport. Par conséquent, il est très gros. L'après-midi, je lis des magazines dans ma chambre ou j'écoute de la musique. Pendant la semaine, quand je rentre à la maison, je fais mes devoirs dans le salon avec ma mère et elle m'aide. Finalement, je me couche dans ma chambre à neuf heures.

Je m'appelle Valentin. Je suis italien. Le matin, je me lève tôt, vers six heures et demie. Ensuite, je me lave et je me brosse les dents dans la salle de bain. Je ne mange rien pour le petit-déjeuner, mais ma sœur Valérie prend des céréales dans la salle à manger avec mon père. Je vais au collège à pied. Je rentre chez moi vers trois heures et demie et je me repose un peu. En général, je regarde la télé dans le salon. Ensuite, je surfe sur internet, Je regarde une série sur Netflix ou des vidéos sur TikTok dans ma chambre. À huit heures, je prépare le repas avec ma mère. Je me couche assez tard, généralement vers dix heures.

Je m'appelle Édouard et j'habite à Nantes. Tous les jours, je me lève à cinq heures du matin. Ensuite, je me douche et je prends le petit-déjeuner sur la terrasse dans le jardin. Je sors de chez moi à sept heures et je vais à l'école à cheval. Quand je rentre à la maison, je tchatte avec mon cousin sur Skype. Il habite en Angleterre depuis cinq ans maintenant. Ensuite, je fais du vélo dans ma rue avec mes deux chiens. Parfois, je regarde des dessins animés et je poste des photos sur Instagram dans la chambre de mon frère. Mon frère Samuel poste des vidéos de ses nouvelles danses sur TikTok. J'aime mon frère car il est amusant et actif. Il danse très bien! Je discute et je joue aux cartes avec lui. Samuel est mon meilleur ami.

1. Answer the following questions about Fabien

a. Where is he from?

b. What animal does he have?

c. What does he do after he wakes up?

d. Why is Joël fat?

e. Where does he do his homework on weekdays?

f. Who helps him with his homework?

g. Where does he go to bed?

2. Find the French for the phrases below in Édouard's text

a. I get up

b. Then I shower

c. I go to school

d. By horse

e. Since five years

f. Uploads videos to TikTok

g. New dances

h. I chat (2)

3. Find Someone Who: which person...

a. wakes up earliest

b. has a family member that likes to dance

c. rides his bike in his street with his two dogs

d. has nothing for breakfast

e. has a really lazy brother

f. prepares food with his mum

g. has a family member who is their best friend

h. goes to school in the most exciting way

4. Find the French for the following phrases/sentences in Valentin's text

a. I am Italian

b. I wake up early

c. I have nothing for breakfast

d. Valérie has cereals

e. In the dining room

f. In the living room

g. I watch TikTok videos

 THE LANGUAGE GYM

Unit 18. Saying what I do at home: WRITING

1. Split sentences

Je discute	repas
Je me repose dans	tôt
Je prépare le	avec ma mère
Je poste des photos	ma chambre
Je fais mes	les dents
Je me lève très	sur Instagram
Je joue sur mon	ordinateur
Je me brosse	devoirs

2. Complete with the correct option

a. Je me lève à six heures du _____.

b. Je joue au foot dans le _____.

c. Je regarde la télé dans le _____.

d. J'écoute de la musique dans ma _____.

e. Je prépare le _____ avec mon père.

f. Je me _____ les dents.

g. Je _____ des dessins animés.

h. Je _____ au collège à cheval.

salon	matin	brosse	chambre
vais	repas	regarde	jardin

3. Spot and correct the grammar and spelling mistakes note: in several cases a word is missing

a. Je ne douche dans le salle de bain.

b. Je déjeune en la cuisine.

c. Dan ma chambre.

d. Je joue sur ordinateur.

e. Je sors de chez moi à huit.

f. Je fais mon devoirs.

g. Je regarde séries sur Netflix.

h. Je au collège à cheval.

i. La chambre mon frère.

4. Complete the words

a. Je d_____ *I have lunch*

b. La cu_____ *The kitchen*

c. Ma _____ *My bedroom*

d. Le _____ *The garage*

e. Je s___ de c____ moi *I leave my house*

f. Dans le _____ *In the living room*

g. La _____ *The dining room*

h. Dans la _____ d_____ b_____
In the bathroom

i. Je _____ des f_____ d_____ la
c_____ d___ m___ f_____
I watch films in my brother's bedroom

5. Guided writing – write 3 short paragraphs in the first person I using the details below

Person	Gets up	Showers	Has breakfast	Goes to school	Evening activity 1	Evening activity 2
Jérôme	6.15	in bathroom	kitchen	with brother	watch tv in living room	prepare food in the kitchen
Maurice	7.30	in shower	dining room	with mother	read book in bedroom	talk to family on Skype
Anne	6.45	in bathroom	living room	with uncle	listen to music in garden	post photos to Instagram

Grammar Time 16: JOUER, (Part 3) FAIRE (Part 3) ALLER (Part 2)

1. Complete with 'fais', 'joue' or 'vais'

a. Je _____ mes devoirs.

b. Je _____ aux échecs.

c. Je _____ en Espagne.

d. Je _____ à la piscine.

e. Je _____ sur mon ordinateur.

f. Je ne_____ jamais au gymnase.

g. Je _____ au tennis.

h. Je ne _____ pas de natation.

3. Complete with the appropriate verb

a. Ma mère _____ à l'église tous les samedis.

b. Ma sœur ne _____ jamais ses devoirs.

c. Nous _____ au basket tous les jours.

d. Mes parents ne _____ pas beaucoup de sport.

e. Mes frères _____ souvent aux échecs.

f. Ma petite amie et moi _____ au collège à pied.

g. Que _____-tu?

h. Où _____-vous?

i. Quel travail _____-tu?

j. Mon cousin _____ au foot avec nous.

k. Mes oncles _____ souvent au stade pour regarder des matchs.

l. Mon père _____ au tennis de temps en temps.

m. En été, mes parents et moi _____ de la voile.

n. Le week-end, mes parents ne _____ rien.

2. Complete with the missing forms of the present indicative of the verbs below

	Faire	Aller	Jouer
je **I**		vais	joue
tu **you**	fais		
il, elle **he/she**			
nous **we**			
vous **you guys**	faites		jouez
ils, elles **they**		vont	

4. Complete with the 'nous' form of jouer/faire/aller

a. _____ au rugby   g. _____ au cricket

b. _____ au collège   h. _____ à la piscine

c. _____ au basket   i. _____ du sport

d. _____ en boîte   j. _____ de la voile

e. _____ au tennis   k. _____ du footing

f. _____ au parc   l. _____ aux échecs

5. Complete with the 'ils' form of jouer/faire/aller

a. _____ au basket   g. _____ à la maison

b. _____ au stade   h. _____ au volley

c. _____ de l'escalade i. _____ au tennis

d. _____ leurs devoirs j. _____ du footing

e. _____ du surf   k. _____ au foot

f. _____ à la plage   l. _____ au cricket

 THE LANGUAGE GYM

Present Indicative of -ER reflexive verbs

	Se laver	Se doucher
je	me lave	me douche
tu	te laves	te douches
il elle	se lave	se douche
nous	nous lavons	nous douchons
vous	vous lavez	vous douchez
ils elles	se lavent	se douchent

USEFUL VOCABULARY

Se raser	To shave
Se baigner	To bathe
Se brosser les dents	To brush one's teeth
Se doucher	To shower
S'appeler	To be called
Se laver	To wash
Se lever	To get up
Se reposer	To relax
Se peigner	To comb one's hair
Se préparer	To get ready

6. Translate into French

a. We often play on the computer.

b. My brother never goes to the gym.

c. My sister plays netball every day.

d. My father never does sport.

e. What job do you guys do?

f. Where do you go after school?

g. My brother and I often play chess.

h. My parents and I go swimming once a week.

i. My brother never goes to church.

j. My best friend goes to the stadium every Saturday.

7. Complete with the correct ending

a. Ma mère s'appell___ Marina.

b. Mon frère ne se lav___ pas.

c. Je me douch___ souvent.

d. Mon père se ras___ tous les jours.

e. Premièrement je me douche, ensuite je me peign___.

f. Nous nous lev_____ tôt le matin.

g. Quand te douch___-tu?

h. Comment t'appell___-tu?

8. Translate into French

a. We get up at six.

b. He showers, then shaves.

c. I shower at around seven.

d. My father never shaves.

e. My brothers never wash.

f. He is called Michel.

g. They get ready.

h. She gets up late.

i. He doesn't brush his teeth.

j. When do you relax?

UNIT 19
My holiday plans
(Talking about future plans for holidays)

In this unit you will learn how to talk about:

- What you intend to do in future holidays
- Where you are going to go
- Where you are going to stay
- Who you are going to travel with
- How it will be
- Means of transport

You will revisit:
- The verb 'aller'
- Free-time activities
- Previously seen adjectives

UNIT 19
My holiday plans

Cet été, je vais aller en vacances en *This summer I am going to go on holiday to* **Nous allons aller en** *We are going to go to*	Allemagne Angleterre Bourgogne Bretagne Espagne	**en avion** *by plane* **en bateau** *by boat* **en car** *by coach* **en voiture** *by car*	
Je vais passer… *I am going to spend* **Nous allons passer…** *We are going to spend*	**une semaine** *1 week* **deux semaines** *2 weeks*	**là-bas** *over there* **avec ma famille** *with my family*	
Je vais rester dans *I am going to stay in* **Nous allons rester dans** *We are going to stay in*	**la maison de ma famille** **un camping** **un hôtel bon marché** *a cheap hotel* **un hôtel de luxe** *a luxury hotel*		**Ce sera ennuyeux** *It will be boring*
Je vais… *I am going to…* **Nous allons…** *We are going to…* **J'aimerais…** **Je voudrais…** *I would like to…* **Nous aimerions…** **Nous voudrions…** *We would like to…*	**acheter des souvenirs** *buy souvenirs* **aller à la plage** *go to the beach* **aller en boîte** *go clubbing* **bronzer** *sunbathe* **danser** *dance* **faire des courses** *go shopping* **faire de la plongée** *go scuba diving* **faire du sport** *do sport* **faire du tourisme** *go sightseeing* **faire du vélo** *go biking* **jouer avec des amis** *play with some friends* **jouer de la guitare** *play the guitar* **manger et dormir** *eat and sleep* **manger de la nourriture délicieuse** *eat delicious food* **me/nous reposer** *rest* **sortir en ville** *go out into town*		**Ce sera amusant** *It will be fun* **Ce sera génial** *It will be great*

Unit 19. My holiday plans: VOCABULARY BUILDING

1. Match up

Je vais aller	I am going to spend
Je vais passer	A campsite
Je vais rester	I am going to go
Bon marché	It will be great
Un camping	I am going to stay
J'aimerais	To buy
Acheter	Cheap
Ce sera génial	I would like to

2. Complete with the missing word

a. Manger et _____ : *To eat and sleep*

b. Je vais me _____ : *I am going to rest*

c. J'_____ aller: *I would like to go*

d. _____ avec mes amis: *To play with my friends*

e. Je _____ dans: *I am going to stay in*

f. _____ ennuyeux: *It will be boring*

g. Nous allons _____ : *We are going to spend*

h. Je vais voyager en _____
I am going to travel by plane

i. Je vais passer deux semaines _____ avec ma
_____ : *I am going to spend two weeks over there with my family*

3. Translate into English

a. Cet été, je vais aller en Italie.

b. Je vais passer trois semaines là-bas.

c. Je vais aller à Bordeaux en avion.

d. Nous allons acheter des souvenirs.

e. J'aimerais sortir en ville.

f. Je vais jouer avec mes amis.

g. Nous aimerions manger et dormir.

h. Je vais me reposer tous les jours.

i. Je vais faire du sport avec mon frère.

4. Broken words

a. Mang____ et dorm_____ : *To eat and sleep*

b. Nous allons _____ : *We are going to stay*

c. Je vais p_____ : *I am going to spend*

d. Je v_____ aller : *I would like to go*

e. Aller à la p_____ : *To go to the beach*

f. F_____ du vélo : *To go biking*

g. B_____ : *To sunbathe*

h. Ce _____ amusant : *It will be fun*

5. 'Aller', 'Jouer' or 'Faire'?

a. _____ des courses

b. _____ à la plage

c. _____ du tourisme

d. _____ au foot

e. _____ de la plongée

f. _____ en boîte

g. _____ du vélo

h. _____ du sport

i. _____ aux échecs

j. _____ de la guitare

6. Bad translation: spot any translation errors and fix them

a. Cet été nous allons aller: *Last summer I am going to go*

b. Je vais aller en Ardèche avec mon père:
I am going to go to Ardèche with my mother

c. Je vais manger et dormir: *I am going to drink and sleep*

d. Je voudrais me reposer une heure: *I would like to rest a bit*

e. Nous allons rester dans un hôtel: *I am going to stay in a hotel*

f. Je vais passer une semaine là-bas:
I am going to spend one week here

g. Nous allons voyager en voiture: *I am going to travel by coach*

h. Je vais rester dans la maison de ma famille:
We are going to stay in my family's house

Unit 19. My holiday plans: READING (Part 1)

Je m'appelle Hugo. Je suis de Cogolin, mais j'habite à Paris. Cet été, je vais aller en vacances dans le sud de l'Espagne, à Cadix. Je vais voyager en voiture avec ma petite amie Alexandra. Nous allons passer quatre semaines là-bas et nous allons aller à la plage tous les jours. Nous allons aussi manger de la nourriture délicieuse. Je ne vais pas faire de tourisme, car c'est ennuyeux. Je préfère bronzer au soleil ou jouer au foot sur le sable.

Je m'appelle Deryk et je suis canadien. Dans ma famille, il y a quatre personnes. Ma personne favorite, c'est ma femme, Anna. Cet été nous allons voyager en Angleterre et après au Québec, au Canada. Je vais me reposer et lire des livres en Angleterre et après je vais faire de la randonnée et sortir avec mes amis au Québec. Anna va faire du vélo et manger de la nourriture délicieuse comme de la 'poutine' (des frites avec du fromage). Ce sera génial!

Je m'appelle Dino. Je suis italien, de Venise. Cet été, je vais aller en vacances au Mexique en avion. Je vais passer deux semaines seul là-bas, et je vais rester dans une caravane sur la plage. Je vais visiter des monuments, des musées et des galeries d'art. Je n'aime pas beaucoup le sport, mais j'adore la culture. Ce sera intéressant.

Je m'appelle Diana. Je suis de Pologne, mais je vis en Chine. Cet eté, je vais voyager à Madagascar avec mon amie Olivia. Je vais voyager en bateau car j'ai beaucoup de temps. Je vais passer cinq semaines là-bas et je vais rester dans un hôtel de luxe. J'adore danser, et donc je vais danser tous les jours. Je vais aussi manger et dormir beaucoup. Je ne vais pas visiter de musées, car c'est très ennuyeux.

1. Find the French for the following in Hugo's text

a. I am from:

b. But I live in:

c. I am going to travel by:

d. With my girlfriend:

e. We are going to spend:

f. Every day:

g. I am not going to:

2. Find the French in Diana's text:

a. By boat:

b. I have a lot of time:

c. I am going to spend:

d. I love to dance:

e. So/therefore:

f. Also:

g. It is very boring:

3. Complete the following statements about Deryk

a. He is from _____

b. His favourite person is _____

c. They will travel to _____ and

_____

d. In Québec, Deryk is going to _____
and _____

e. Anna is going to _____ and

_____

4. List any 8 details about Dino (in 3rd person) in English

1.

2.

3.

4.

5.

6.

7.

8.

5. Find someone who…

a. …likes being out at sea for long periods

b. …loves learning about culture

c. ...prefers the beach to sightseeing

d. …has opposite interests to Dino

e. …is going to travel by car

Unit 19. My holiday plans: READING (Part 2)

Je m'appelle Bixente. Je suis de Ghéthary. J'ai une tortue chez moi. Elle est très lente et très grosse, mais je l'adore. C'est ma meilleure amie. Cet été, je vais aller en vacances à Concarneau en Bretagne avec ma famille. Je vais voyager en avion et ensuite en voiture. Nous allons passer trois semaines sur la côte et nous allons rester dans un hôtel de luxe. Ce sera très amusant! Après nous allons aller en voiture à Lorient et nous allons voir le Festival Interceltique. Je vais écouter de la musique bretonne et manger beaucoup de délicieux fruits de mer; j'adore les crevettes et le crabe! Je vais aussi faire les magasins tous les jours et je vais acheter des vêtements.

Je m'appelle Fred. Je suis de Saint-Leu sur l'île de la Réunion. Cet été, je vais aller en vacances à Chamonix dans les Alpes avec mon ami Éric. Nous allons voyager en avion et passer deux semaines là-bas. À Chamonix, nous allons visiter un site unique: l'Aiguille du Midi. Ce sera très impressionnant et divertissant. Nous allons aussi faire des randonnées dans la montagne. Ce sera dur, mais génial. Un jour, je voudrais me reposer et jouer de la guitare. J'adore chanter et Éric aime jouer du piano. Notre groupe favori s'appelle Queen. Ma musique préférée, c'est le rock!

Je m'appelle Joséphine et j'habite à Mulhouse, dans l'est de la France. Cet été, je vais voyager à Embrun, dans le sud-est de la France. Je vais voyager en train et ensuite en voiture. Je vais passer deux semaines là-bas et je vais rester dans un hôtel bon marché. À Embrun, je voudrais nager dans le lac tous les jours et je vais peut-être essayer le kayak. J'irai aussi à la montagne pour faire des randonnée et je vais aussi essayer le parapente, ce sera génial! J'ai une amie qui s'appelle Alice. Nous allons discuter et bronzer ensemble sur les bords du lac, ce sera relaxant. Le soir, nous allons manger au restaurant et aller en boîte, ce sera amusant et divertissant.

1. Answer the following questions about Bixente

a. Where is he from?

b. What animal does he have?

c. Who will he go on holiday with?

d. Where will they stay?

e. How will they get to Concarneau?

f. What will he do in Lorient?

g. What will he do every day?

2. Find the French in Joséphine's text

a. this summer

b. and then

c. which is called

d. lake

e. paragliding

f. entertaining

g. to try

h. sunbathe together

3. Find the French for the following phrases/sentences in Fred's text

a. My friend Éric

b. Two weeks

c. It will be very impressive

d. It will be tough

e. I would like to rest

f. To play the guitar

g. Our favourite group

h. Rock music

4. Find someone who...

a. ...is going to travel south?

b. ...has a friend who is a musician?

c. ...has a slow moving pet?

d. ...is going to be walking in the mountains?

e. ...is going to try a new sport?

f. ...is going to visit a famous mountain peak?

g. ...lives on an island

h. ...is going to eat seafood?

 THE LANGUAGE GYM

Unit 19. My holiday plans: TRANSLATION/WRITING

1. Gapped translation

a. *I am going to go on holiday:* **Je vais aller en _____**

b. *I am going to travel by car:* **Je vais voyager en _____**

c. *We are going to spend one week over there:*

Nous allons _____ une semaine _____

d. *I am going to stay in a cheap hotel:*

___ _____ rester dans un hôtel _____ _____

e. *We are going to eat and sleep every day:*

Nous allons manger et _____ tous les _____

f. *If the weather is nice, I am going to go to the beach:*

S'il fait _____, je vais aller à la _____

g. *I am going to go shopping:* **Je vais faire les _____**

2. Translate to English

a. Manger

b. Acheter

c. Se reposer

d. Faire du tourisme

e. Aller à la plage

f. Tous les jours

g. En avion

h. Faire de la plongée

i. Sortir en ville

3. Spot and correct the grammar and spelling mistakes note: in several cases a word is missing

a. Je vais faire sport.

b. Je passer une semaine làbas.

c. Je vais rester dans un hôtel luxe.

d. Nous allons rester dans une hotel.

e. Je voudrais jouer a un foot.

f. Nous allons sortir au center-ville.

g. Je vais vais à la plage.

h. Je vais jouer à mes amis.

4. Categories: Positive or Negative?
Write P or N

a. Ce sera amusant: **P**

b. Ce sera ennuyeux:

c. Ce sera agréable:

d. Ce sera relaxant:

e. Ce sera intéressant:

f. Ce sera horrible:

g. Ce sera nul:

h. Ce sera dégoûtant:

i. Ce sera fascinant:

j. Ce sera impressionnant:

5. Translate into French

a. I am going to rest.

b. I am going to go scuba diving.

c. We are going to go to the beach.

d. I am going to sunbathe.

e. I would like to go sightseeing.

f. I am going to stay in…

g. A cheap hotel.

h. We are going to spend two weeks…

i. I am going to go over there by plane.

j. It will be fun.

Revision Quickie 6: Daily Routine/House/Home life/Holidays

1. Match-up

Dans la banlieue	In the garden
Dans la salle de bain	In the living room
Dans la cuisine	In my bedroom
Dans ma maison	In my house
Dans le jardin	In the shower
Dans ma chambre	In the dining room
Dans la salle à manger	In the bathroom
Dans la douche	In the kitchen
Dans le salon	On the outskirts

2. Complete with the missing letters

a. Je me dou_____ *I shower*

b. Je me l_____ *I get up*

c. Je re_____ la télé *I watch telly*

d. Je l_____ des BD *I read comics*

e. Je s_____ de chez moi *I leave home*

f. J'_____ au collège *I arrive at school*

g. Je pr_____ le bus *I catch the bus*

h. Je m'h_____ *I get dressed*

i. Je d_____ *I have lunch*

3. Spot and correct any of the sentences below which do not make sense

a. Je me douche dans le frigo.

b. Je mange dans la douche.

c. Je prépare le repas dans ma chambre.

d. Je me lave les cheveux dans le salon.

e. Je vais dans ma chambre en bus.

f. Je joue au ping-pong avec mon frère.

g. Le sofa est dans la cuisine.

h. Je regarde la télé dans le jardin.

i. Je dors dans l'armoire.

j. Je gare la voiture dans le salon.

4. Split sentences

Je regarde	le bus
J'écoute	céréales
Je lis	la télé
Je prends	un café
Je mange des	de la musique
Je vais aller au	des magazines
Je bois	devoirs
Je poste des photos	Japon en avion
Je fais mes	sur Instagram
Je range	aux cartes
Je travaille sur	ma chambre
Je joue	mon ordinateur

5. Match the opposites

Bon	Malsain
Sympathique	Mauvais
Facile	Beau
Amusant	Antipathique
Sain	Difficile
Moche	Ennuyeux
Cher	Rapide
Lent	Grand
Souvent	Bon marché
Jamais	Rarement
Petit	Toujours

6. Complete with the missing words

a. Je vais aller au Japon _____ avion.

b. Je vais aller en Italie _____ mes parents.

c. Je ne joue jamais _____ foot.

d. Je déteste _____ cricket.

e. Je reste dans un hôtel _____ luxe.

f. Je vais au parc une fois _____ semaine.

g. Je surfe _____ internet.

h. Je poste des photos _____ Instagram.

7. Draw a line in between each word

a. Jaimebeaucoupjoueraubasket

b. Jeregardelatéléetjécoutedelamusique

c. Pendantmontempslibrejejoueauxjeuxvidéos

d. JevaisalleronAllemagneenvoiture

e. Jevaisresterdansunhôteldeluxe

f. Lematinjevaisalleràlaplage

g. Jevaisallerenboîtesamedi

h. Jenefaisjamaismesdevoirs

8. Spot the translation mistakes and correct them

a. Je me lève tôt: *I go to bed early*

b. Je déteste le basket: *I hate volleyball*

c. Je vais aller à la piscine: *I am going to go to the beach*

d. Nous n'allons rien faire: *I am not going to do anything*

e. Je vais nager: *I am going to run*

f. Je vais voyager en voiture: *I am going to travel by plane*

g. Je vais rester dans un hôtel de luxe:

I am going to stay in a cheap hotel

h. Je vais regarder un film: *I am going to watch a series*

9. Translate into English:

a. Je prends l'avion:

b. Je vais aller:

c. Je vais rester:

d. Je me lave:

e. Je regarde un film:

f. Je range ma chambre:

g. Je mange des légumes:

h. J'aime les œufs:

i. Je ne fais rien:

j. Je travaille sur mon ordinateur:

10. Translate into English

a. Je me douche et je prends le petit-déjeuner.

b. Demain, je vais aller au Japon.

c. Je range ma chambre tous les jours.

d. Je ne joue jamais au basket.

e. Je me lève tôt.

f. Je mange beaucoup au petit-déjeuner.

g. Je vais aller en Italie en voiture.

h. Pendant mon temps libre, je lis des livres.

i. Je passe beaucoup de temps sur internet.

11. Translate into French

a. I have dinner: Je _ _ _ _

b. I watch: Je _ _ _ _ _ _ _

c. I do: Je _ _ _ _

d. I tidy up: Je _ _ _ _ _

e. I read: Je _ _ _

f. I work: Je _ _ _ _ _ _ _ _ _

g. I rest: Je me _ _ _ _ _ _

h. I go: Je _ _ _ _

i. I take: Je _ _ _ _ _ _

Question Skills 4: Daily routine/House/Home life/Holidays

1. Complete the questions with the correct option

a. _____ heure tu te lèves?

b. _____ tu t'appelles?

c. _____ fais-tu après le collège?

d. _____ d'heures passes-tu sur ton ordinateur?

e. _____ joues-tu à la Playstation?

f. _____ tu ne fais pas plus de sport?

g. _____ vas-tu le vendredi soir?

h. _____ est ta pièce préférée?

Où	À quelle	Combien	Que
Pourquoi	Quelle	Comment	Avec qui

2. Split questions

À quelle heure	tu ne joues pas au foot avec nous?
Que manges-tu	vas-tu au gymnase par semaine?
Que	rentres-tu chez toi?
Avec	fais-tu du footing?
Pourquoi	pour le petit-déjeuner?
Combien de fois	qui joues-tu aux échecs?
Où	fais-tu pendant le week-end?
Comment passes-tu	tes parents à la maison?
Tu aides	ton temps libre?

3. Match each statement below to one of the questions included in activity 1 above

a. Deux ou trois.

b. Je m'appelle Bertrand.

c. Mon petit frère.

d. Vers six heures.

e. Je vais en boîte avec mon meilleur ami.

f. Je rentre à la maison.

g. Car je suis paresseux et je n'ai pas le temps.

h. Ma chambre bien sûr!

4. Translate into French

a. Who?

b. When?

c. Who with?

d. Why?

e. How much?

f. How?

g. Which ones?

h. Where?

i. Do you do…?

j. Can you…?

k. Where is…?

l. How many hours?

m. How many people?

5. Translate

a. Where is your bedroom?

b. Where do you go after school?

c. What do you do in your free time?

d. Until what time do you study?

e. How long do you spend on the internet?

f. What is your favourite pastime?

g. What do you do to help in the house?

THE LANGUAGE GYM

VOCABULARY TESTS

On the following pages you will find one vocabulary test for every unit in the book. You could set them as class assessments or as homework at the end of a unit. Students could also use them to practice independently.

1a. Translate the following sentences (worth one point each) into French

What is your name?	
My name is Paul	
How old are you?	
I am five years old	
I am seven years old	
I am nine years old	
I am ten years old	
I am eleven years old	
I am twelve years old	
I am thirteen years old	
Score	**/10**

1b. Translate the following sentences (worth two points each) into French

What is your brother called?	
What is your sister called?	
My brother is called Mathieu	
My sister is fourteen years old	
My brother is fifteen years old	
I don't have any brothers or sisters	
My name is Jean and I am French	
I have a brother who is called Philippe	
I live in the capital of Japan	
I live in the capital of France	
Score	**/20**

THE LANGUAGE GYM

1a. Translate the following sentences (worth one point each) into French

My name is Serge	
I am eleven years old	
I am fifteen years old	
I am eighteen years old	
The 3rd May	
The 4th April	
The 5th June	
The 6th September	
The 10th October	
The 8th July	
Score	**/10**

1b. Translate the following sentences (worth two points each) into French

I am 17. My birthday is on 21st June.	
My brother is called Jules. He is 19.	
My sister is called Marie. She is 22.	
My brother's birthday is on 23rd March.	
My name is Philippe. I am 15. My birthday is on 27th July.	
My name is Grégoire. I am 18. My birthday is on 30th June.	
When is your birthday?	
Is your birthday in October or November?	
My brother is called Pierre. His birthday is on 31st January.	
Is your birthday in May or June?	
Score	**/20**

1a. Translate the following sentences (worth one point each) into French

Black hair	
Light brown hair	
Blond hair	
Blue eyes	
My name is Léa	
I am 12 years old	
I have long hair	
I have short hair	
I have green eyes	
I have brown eyes	
Score	**/10**

1b. Translate the following sentences (worth two points each) into French

I have grey hair and green eyes.	
I have red straight hair.	
I have curly white hair.	
I have light brown hair and brown eyes.	
I wear glasses and have spikey hair.	
I don't wear glasses and I have a beard.	
My brother has blond hair and he has a moustache.	
My brother is 22 years old and has shaved hair.	
Do you wear glasses?	
My sister has blue eyes and wavy black hair.	
Score	**/20**

1a. Translate the following sentences (worth one point each) into French

My name is	
I am from	
I live in	
In a house	
In a modern building	
In an old building	
On the outskirts	
In the centre	
On the coast	
In Biarritz	
Score	**/10**

1b. Translate the following sentences (worth two points each) into French

My brother is called Paul.	
My sister is called Alexandra.	
I live in an old building.	
I live in a modern building.	
I live in a beautiful house on the coast.	
I live in an old house in the centre.	
I am from Paris, but I live in the centre of Casablanca.	
I am 15 years old and I am French.	
I am French, from Biarritz, but I live in Nouméa, in New Caledonia.	
I live in a small apartment in the countryside.	
Score	**/20**

1a. Translate the following sentences (worth one point each) into French	
My younger brother	
My older brother	
My older sister	
My younger sister	
My father	
My mother	
My uncle	
My aunt	
My male cousin	
My female cousin	
Score	**/10**

1b. Translate the following sentences (worth two points each) into French	
In my family there are four people.	
My father, my mother and my two brothers.	
I don't get along with my older brother.	
My older sister is 22.	
My younger sister is 16.	
My grandfather is 78.	
My grandmother is 67.	
My uncle is 54.	
My aunt is 44.	
My female cousin is 17.	
Score	**/20**

UNIT 6 "Describing myself and my family members"   TOTAL SCORE: /30

1a. Translate the following sentences (worth one point each) into French

Tall (masculine)	
Short (feminine)	
Ugly (masculine)	
Good-looking (masculine)	
Generous (masculine)	
Boring (feminine)	
Intelligent (masculine)	
Muscular (masculine)	
Kind (feminine)	
Fat (masculine)	
Score	**/10**

1b. Translate the following sentences (worth two points each) into French

My mother is strict and boring.	
My father is stubborn and unfriendly.	
My older sister is intelligent and hard-working.	
My younger sister is sporty.	
In my family, I have five people.	
I get along with my older sister because she is nice.	
I don't get along with my younger sister because she is annoying.	
I love my grandparents because they are funny and generous..	
What are your parents like?	
My uncle and my aunt are fifty and I don't get along with them.	
Score	**/20**

THE LANGUAGE GYM

170

1a. Translate the following sentences (worth one point each) into French

A horse	
A rabbit	
A dog	
A turtle	
A bird	
A parrot	
A duck	
A guinea pig	
A cat	
A mouse	
Score	**/10**

1b. Translate the following sentences (worth three points each) into French

I have a white horse.	
I have a green turtle.	
At home we have two fish.	
My sister has a spider.	
I don't have pets.	
My friend Pierre has a blue bird.	
My cat is very fat.	
I have a snake that is called Boa.	
My duck is funny and noisy.	
How many pets do you have at home?	
Score	**/30**

1a. Translate the following sentences (worth one point each) into French

He is a male cook.	
He is a journalist.	
She is a waitress.	
She is a nurse.	
He is a househusband.	
She is a doctor.	
He is a teacher.	
She is a businesswoman.	
He is a hairdresser.	
She is a farmer.	
Score	/10

1b. Translate the following sentences (worth three points each) into French

My uncle is a cook.	
My mother is a nurse.	
My grandparents don't work.	
My sister works as a teacher.	
My aunt is an actress.	
My (male) cousin is a student.	
My cousins are lawyers.	
He doesn't like it because it is hard.	
He likes it because it is gratifying.	
He hates it because it is stressful.	
Score	/30

1a. Translate the following sentences (worth two points each) into French

He is taller than me.	
He is more generous than her.	
She is less fat than him.	
He is slimmer than her.	
She is better looking than him.	
She is more talkative than me.	
I am more funny than him.	
My dog is less noisy.	
My rabbit is more fun.	
She is as talkative as me.	
Score	**/20**

1b. Translate the following sentences (worth 3 points each) into French

My brother is stronger than me.	
My mother is shorter than my father.	
My uncle is better looking than my father.	
My older sister is more talkative than my younger sister.	
My sister and I are taller than my cousins.	
My grandfather is less strict than my grandmother.	
My friend Paul is friendlier than my friend Philippe.	
My rabbit is bigger than my duck.	
My cat is fatter than my dog.	
My mouse is faster than my turtle.	
Score	**/30**

 **THE LANGUAGE GYM**

1a. Translate the following sentences (worth one point each) into French

I have a pen	
I have a ruler	
I have a rubber	
In my bag	
In my pencil case	
My friend Paul	
Pierre has	
I don't have	
A purple exercise book	
A yellow pencil sharpener	
Score	**/10**

1b. Translate the following sentences (worth three points each) into French

In my bag I have four books.	
I have a yellow pencil case.	
I have a red bag.	
I don't have black felt tip pens.	
There are two blue pens.	
My friend Paul has a pencil sharpener.	
Do you guys have a rubber?	
Do you have a red pen?	
Is there a ruler in your pencil case?	
What is there in your bag?	
Score	**/30**

1a. Translate the following sentences (worth three points each) into French

I don't like milk.	
I love meat.	
I don't like fish much.	
I hate chicken.	
Fruit is tasty.	
Honey is healthy.	
I prefer mineral water.	
Milk is disgusting.	
Chocolate is delicious.	
Cheese is unhealthy.	
Score	**/30**

1b. Translate the following sentences (worth five points each) into French

I love chocolate because it is delicious.	
I like apples a lot because they are healthy.	
I don't like red meat because it is unhealthy.	
I don't like sausages because they are unhealthy.	
I love fish with French fries.	
I hate seafood because it is disgusting.	
I like fruit because it is healthy and delicious.	
I like spicy chicken with vegetables.	
I like eggs because they are rich in protein.	
Roast chicken is tastier than fried fish.	
Score	**/50**

1a. Translate the following sentences (worth one point each) into French

I have breakfast	
I have lunch	
I have 'snack'	
I have dinner	
Delicious	
Healthy	
Disgusting	
Refreshing	
Hard	
Sweet	
Score	**/10**

1b. Translate the following sentences (worth three points each) into French

I eat eggs and drink coffee for breakfast.	
I have seafood for lunch.	
I never have dinner.	
For snack I have bread with butter.	
In the morning I usually eat fruit.	
I love meat because it is tasty.	
From time to time I eat cheese.	
In the evening I eat little.	
We eat a lot of meat and fish.	
I don't often eat sweets.	
Score	**/30**

1a. Translate the following sentences (worth two points each) into French

A red skirt	
A blue suit	
A green scarf	
Black trousers	
A white shirt	
A brown hat	
A yellow T-shirt	
Blue jeans	
A purple tie	
Grey shoes	
Score	**/20**

1b. Translate the following sentences (worth three points each) into French

I often wear a black baseball cap.	
At home I wear a blue track suit.	
At school we wear a green uniform.	
At the beach I wear a red bathing suit.	
My sister always wears jeans.	
My brother never wears a watch.	
My mother wears branded clothes.	
I very rarely wear suits.	
My girlfriend wears a pretty dress.	
My brothers always wear trainers.	
Score	**/30**

THE LANGUAGE GYM

UNIT 14 "Talking about free time"   TOTAL SCORE: /70

1a. Translate the following sentences (worth two points each) into French

I do my homework.	
I play football.	
I go rock climbing.	
I go cycling.	
I go hiking.	
I go to the swimming pool.	
I do sport.	
I do horse riding.	
I play tennis.	
I go to the beach.	
Score	**/20**

1b. Translate the following sentences (worth five points each) into French

I never play basketball because it is boring.	
I play on the Playstation with my friends.	
My father and I go fishing from time to time.	
My brother and I go to the gym every day.	
I go to the gym and I go jogging every day.	
When the weather is nice, we go hiking.	
When the weather is bad, I play chess.	
My father goes swimming at the weekend.	
My younger brothers go to the park after school.	
In my free time, I go rock climbing or go to my friend's house.	
Score	**/50**

1a. Translate the following sentences (worth two points each) into French

When the weather is nice.	
When the weather is bad.	
When it is sunny.	
When it is cold.	
When it is hot.	
I go skiing.	
I play with my friends.	
I go to the mall.	
I go to the gym.	
I go on a bike ride.	
Score	**/20**

1b. Translate the following sentences (worth four points each) into French

When the weather is nice, I go jogging.	
When it rains, we go to the sports centre and we play tennis.	
At the weekend, I do my homework and a bit of sport.	
When it is hot, she goes to the beach or goes cycling.	
When I have time, I go jogging with my father.	
When there are storms, we stay at home and play cards.	
When the sky is clear, they go to the park.	
On Fridays and Saturdays, I go clubbing with my girlfriend.	
We never do sport. We play on the computer or on the Playstation.	
When it snows, we go to the mountain and ski.	
Score	**/40**

1a. Translate the following sentences (worth one point each) into French

I get up	
I have breakfast	
I eat	
I drink	
I go to bed	
Around six o'clock	
I rest	
At noon	
At midnight	
I do my homework	
Score	**/10**

1b. Translate the following sentences (worth three points each) into French

Around 7.00 in the morning, I have breakfast.	
I shower, then I get dressed.	
I eat, then I brush my teeth.	
Around 8 o'clock in the evening, I have dinner.	
I go to school by bus.	
I watch television in my room.	
I go back home at 4.30.	
From 6 to 7 I play on the computer.	
Afterwards, around 11.30, I go to bed.	
My daily routine is simple.	
Score	**/30**

1a. Translate the following sentences (worth one point each) into French

I live	
In a new house	
In an old house	
In a small house	
In a big house	
On the coast	
In the mountains	
In an ugly apartment	
On the outskirts	
In the centre of town	
Score	/10

1b. Translate the following sentences (worth three points each) into French

In my house there are four rooms.	
My favourite room is the kitchen.	
I like to rest in the living room.	
In my apartment there are seven rooms.	
My parents live in a big house.	
My uncle lives in a small house.	
We live near the coast.	
My friend Paul lives on a farm.	
My cousins live in Bayonne.	
My parents and I live in a cosy house.	
Score	/30

1a. Translate the following sentences (worth one point each) into French

I chat with my mother.	
I play on the Playstation.	
I read magazines.	
I read comics.	
I watch films.	
I listen to music.	
I rest.	
I do my homework.	
I go on a bike ride.	
I leave the house.	
Score	**/10**

1b. Translate the following sentences (worth three points each) into French

I never tidy up my room.	
I rarely help my parents.	
I brush my teeth three times a week.	
I upload many photos onto Instagram.	
Every day I watch series on Netflix.	
I have breakfast at around 7.30.	
After school, I rest in the garden.	
When I have time, I play with my brother.	
Usually, I leave home at 8 o'clock.	
From time to time, I watch a movie.	
Score	**/30**

1a. Translate the following sentences (worth two points each) into French

I am going to go	
I am going to stay	
I am going to play	
I am going to eat	
I am going to drink	
I am going to rest	
I am going to go sightseeing	
I am going to go to the beach	
I am going to do sport	
I am going to dance	
Score	**/20**

1b. Translate the following sentences (worth five points each) into French

We are going to buy souvenirs and clothes.	
I am going to stay in a cheap hotel near the beach.	
We are going to stay there for three weeks.	
I am going to spend two weeks there with my family.	
We are going to go on holiday to Reunion Island tomorrow.	
We are going to Spain for two weeks and we are going to travel by plane.	
I would like to do sport, go to the beach and dance.	
We are going to spend three weeks in Italy, we will stay in a caravan.	
We are going to go and stay in a luxury hotel near the beach.	
We are going to go sightseeing and shopping every day.	
Score	**/50**

The End

We hope you have enjoyed using this workbook and found it useful!

As many of you will appreciate, the penguin is a fantastic animal. At Language Gym, we hold it as a symbol of resilience, bravery and good humour; able to thrive in the harshest possible environments, and with, arguably the best gait in the animal kingdom (black panther or penguin, you choose). There are several hidden penguins (pictures)throughout this book, did you spot them all?

The Language Gym Team